P9-CLH-951

PLATO'S PHILEBUS

PLATO'S PHILEBUS

*Translated with an Introduction
and Commentary by*

R. HACKFORTH, F.B.A.

*formerly Emeritus Professor of Ancient Philosophy
in the University of Cambridge*

CAMBRIDGE
AT THE UNIVERSITY PRESS
1972

Published by the Syndics of the Cambridge University Press
Bentley House, 200 Euston Road, London NW1 2DB
American Branch: 32 East 57th Street, New York, N.Y. 10022

ISBN: 0 521 08460 1   Clothbound
0 521 09704 5   Paperback

First published 1945 (under the title *Plato's Examination of Pleasure*)
Reprinted 1958, 1972

First printed in Great Britain
at the University Printing House, Cambridge

Reprinted in the United States of America

CONTENTS

Preface   *page* vii

INTRODUCTION   1

PHILEBUS: TRANSLATION AND COMMENTARY

11 A–12 B Statement of the issue. The Good for Man   12

12 B–13 D Pleasure as a generic unity, containing a variety of
            species   14

13 E–15 C The Problem of the One and the Many   17

15 D–17 A Dialectic in relation to the One-Many problem   20

17 A–18 D Illustrations of Limit and Unlimited   24

18 D–20 C Interlude   29

20 C–22 C The good life cannot consist exclusively either of
            Pleasure or of Intelligence   31

22 C–23 B Which component of the Mixed Life is the cause of
            its being good? Transition to a metaphysical
            argument   36

23 C–26 D Fourfold classification of all existents   37

26 E–31 B The affinity of Intelligence to the Cosmic Cause,
            and to the cause of goodness in the Mixed Life   49

31 B–32 B Pleasure as replenishment of wastage   58

32 B–36 C Pleasures of anticipation; the part played in them by
            sensation, memory and desire   61

36 C–38 A True and false pleasures   69

38 A–40 E The connexion between False Judgment and False
            Pleasure   72

40 E–42 C A second type of false pleasures, due to error in
            respect of hedonic magnitude   77

42 C–44 A A third type of false pleasures and pains, due to
            non-recognition of a neutral condition   81

44 A–47 B Are any pleasures true? Examination of the extreme
            anti-hedonist position, beginning with mixed
            bodily pleasures   85

47 B–50 E Mixed pleasures of Body and Soul, and of Soul alone.
            Examination of malice, especially as felt by the
            spectator of comedy   92

50 E–52 B Types of true pleasures ᏏᎧᎩᎧᏝ   98

52 C–53 C Purity, not magnitude or intensity, is the mark of truth — 102

53 C–55 A Pleasure as process: the contrast of means and end — 105

55 B–C The common-sense attitude towards Hedonism — 111

55 C–59 C Classification of forms of knowledge — 113

59 C–61 C Recapitulation of earlier conclusions about the Good Life. It is a good mixture, but in what does its goodness consist? — 122

61 D–64 A What kinds of knowledge and of pleasure are admissible in the Good Life? — 127

64 A–66 A Goodness is revealed in the Mixed Life under three forms, Beauty, Proportion and Truth, to each of which Intelligence is more akin than Pleasure — 132

66 A–67 B Fivefold classification of goods, in which pleasures are relegated to the lowest place — 137

Additional Note — 142

Index of Proper Names — 144

PREFACE

On 4 January 1943, when the manuscript of this book was just completed, I heard of the death, the day before, of F. M. Cornford. It will be obvious that I owe a great debt to that fine scholar and interpreter of Plato; it was indeed at his suggestion that I turned to the *Philebus*, and without his encouragement I should probably not have carried through my task.

Anyone who tries to interpret a Platonic dialogue must gratefully acknowledge his obligation to Professor A. E. Taylor. Another living scholar to whom I am much indebted is Dr R. G. Bury, the most recent English editor of the dialogue; the fact that his edition appeared nearly half-a-century ago may help to excuse me for attempting what is, from one point of view, a supplement to his work.

Amongst foreign scholars I have probably derived most help from the writings of Diès, Friedländer, and Constantin Ritter. I have consulted no translation save the German version by Apelt, and have followed Burnet's text, except where noted.

That I have not attempted a full-dress commentary in the traditional style is due partly to my disinclination for the purely philological labour involved, partly to the existence of Dr Bury's book, in which such labour has been so fruitfully expended. I believe, however, that there are many students nowadays who prefer interpretation of a work of ancient philosophy to be offered in a more or less continuous form, or in what approximates to a running commentary, rather than in footnotes to a text or translation. Footnotes cannot indeed be avoided; but I have tried to limit them to essentials.

I am especially grateful to my friend Mr F. H. Sandbach for reading the whole of the translation in manuscript, and for making valuable corrections and suggestions. I have been helped on various points by Dr A. B. Cook, Professor D. S. Robertson, and Mr S. G. Campbell. My thanks are also due to the careful readers of the University Press.

R. HACKFORTH

July 1944

INTRODUCTION

There is general agreement nowadays that the six dialogues, *Sophist*, *Statesman*, *Philebus*, *Timaeus*, *Critias*, *Laws*, were composed in the last two decades of Plato's life, and that the two first named were the first written, the *Laws* the last. The opening words of the *Sophist* link it formally to the *Theaetetus*, a work generally thought to have been written shortly after the death in battle (in 369 B.C.) of the brilliant mathematician after whom it is named; but although 368 or 367 may thus be taken as a *terminus a quo* for the six dialogues, it is difficult to determine the date of any of them more precisely. From the fact that in the *Sophist* Plato for the first time deliberately adopts the Isocratean fashion of avoiding hiatus it has been argued that there was a considerable gap in his literary activity between *Theaetetus* and *Sophist*, and that the interruption may have been caused by his preoccupation with Syracusan politics in the years 367–360. But of the two visits to Syracuse, in 367 and 361, neither seems to have lasted as much as a year; and we may guess that Plato was not more distracted by Sicilian affairs in the interval between these visits than after his final return to Athens in 360, when the storm was blowing up which burst in 357 with Dion's return to Sicily and his expulsion of Dionysius II by force of arms. Indeed, if preoccupation with Dionysius and Dion deterred Plato from the composition of further dialogues, he would hardly have composed the *Sophist* until 352, the probable date of the eighth Epistle.

There is perhaps rather more possibility of approximating to the date of the *Statesman*, which is formally attached to the *Sophist* just as the *Sophist* is to the *Theaetetus*. In that dialogue we seem to see Plato arguing with himself on the relative merits of autocracy and constitutional government. Ostensibly there is a clear answer given: the rule of one man, guided by his own wisdom and unrestricted by laws, is ideally the right form of government; but since the ideally wise ruler is nowhere to be found,[1] the best practical possibility of good government lies in monarchy tempered by the rule of law. Yet we are more than two-thirds of the way through the dialogue before the merits of the law-states begin to be discussed; and it may be conjectured that the reason for their discussion, and for the elaboration of an order of merit for the 'imitations' of the ideal state, itself now deemed impossible, was

[1] *Pol.* 301 D νῦν δέ γε ὁπότε οὐκ ἔστι γιγνόμενος...ἐν ταῖς πόλεσι βασιλεύς...τό τε σῶμα εὐθὺς καὶ τὴν ψυχὴν διαφέρων εἰς κτλ.

the final shattering of Plato's hopes ot making Dionysius a philosopher-king. Those hopes were shattered by his experiences at Syracuse in 361–360: hence it is possible that the *Statesman* was begun just before, and finished just after the final visit to Syracuse.

The *Sophist* and *Statesman* were planned as the first two dialogues of a trilogy,[1] to be completed by the *Philosopher*. That the third dialogue was never written may have been due to the same cause that made the *Statesman* end as it does. We may be fairly sure that, when he began the *Sophist*, Plato intended to show that sophist, statesman and philosopher are not one nor three but two;[2] for he had not then abandoned— nor did he ever abandon as an ideal—the state of the philosophic ruler or rulers described in the *Republic*. The philosopher, however, was to have a dialogue to himself, in which it would be shown in detail (as in *Rep.* VI–VII) what the knowledge desiderated for the ruler in the *Statesman* was, and how his political activity was to reflect his knowledge of reality.[3] It is easy to understand that when Plato became convinced of the improbability of the philosophic statesman ever appearing on earth, he had not the heart to complete his ideal account.

Did he thereupon project and start work on another unfinished trilogy,[4] *Timaeus, Critias, ⟨Hermocrates⟩*? Or did he now write the *Philebus*? The question cannot be answered with certainty, perhaps not even with probability. It is of course possible that the *Philebus* was composed concurrently with the *Timaeus* or *Critias*, just as it is believed by some scholars that the *Parmenides* and *Theaetetus* were written together; it is in a sense, as we shall see, a *pièce d'occasion*, and as such Plato may have interrupted his large-scale project in order to write it. But on the assumption that one or the other (for convenience I speak of *Timaeus* and *Critias* as a single work) must have been composed first, arguments have been found for the priority of each: all, I think, far from cogent: but, such as they are, they seem rather in favour of the *Philebus* being the later work.[5] There are at least three points on which

---

[1] See *Soph.* 253 E, *Pol.* 257 A–C, 258 A; Cornford, *Plato's Theory of Knowledge*, p. 168. Henry Jackson rejects the idea of a trilogy (*J. Ph.* xv, pp. 282 ff.).

[2] This is probably hinted at *Soph.* 217 A: unless interpreted thus, Socrates's question 'Are they one, two, or three?' seems pointless.

[3] For a somewhat different conjecture as to the contents of the *Philosopher* see Cornford, *PTK*, p. 169.

[4] I agree with Cornford (*Plato's Cosmology*, p. 2), against the doubts of Taylor (*Comm. on Timaeus*, p. 14), that *Critias* 108 B makes it certain that a dialogue *Hermocrates* was planned.

[5] So Bury, Taylor and (implicitly) Bäumker (*Prob. der Materie*, pp. 193–6: Taylor's reference to p. 130 of this work seems to be a wrong reference).

the pronouncements of the two works are identical or closely similar, (1) the Cosmic Reason (νοῦς = τὸ δημιουργοῦν in *Philebus* and the Demiurge[1] in *Timaeus*, (2) the opposition of Unlimited and Limit in *Philebus* and that of pre-cosmic chaos and the εἴδη καὶ ἀριθμοί by which it is ordered in *Timaeus*, (3) the essentially similar replenishment-depletion formula for pleasure and pain in the two dialogues. It might be expected that careful examination of the two on these three points would enable us to decide, with at least reasonable assurance, on the question of priority; but I have not found it so.[2] Nor can I find any significance in the comparative figures for avoidance of hiatus (1·1 in *Timaeus* and 3·7 in *Philebus* per Didot page[3]); they only show that he was more careful in one dialogue than in the other, and carefulness may precede carelessness as well as succeed it.

The question is not perhaps of very great moment, but I am tentatively in favour of assigning priority to the *Philebus* on the following ground. The choice of Hermocrates, the distinguished soldier-statesman of Syracuse, as the leading speaker in the final part of the *Timaeus* trilogy suggests that Plato had in mind, when he began the *Timaeus*, a scheme of military and political organisation of which the outlines at least were clear in his mind; but that they should have been sufficiently clear soon after the disillusion of 360 seems improbable; a more likely time would be after the murder of Dion in 354, when, as the seventh and eighth Epistles show, his mind was busily engaged on schemes for the political salvation of Sicily in view of the menace of Carthaginians and Oscans.[4] It would be particularly appropriate that one of the greatest Syracusans of the fifth century should propound advice applicable to his compatriots of the fourth.

It is not relevant to our purpose to speculate why the *Hermocrates* was never written, though we may guess that the death of Hipparinus in 350 and the discomfiture of the friends of Dion finally quenched Plato's hopes for Sicily. There is however some ground for believing that the *Laws*, whose composition was to occupy the few remaining years of

---

[1] I do not intend by this parallel to deny the partly mythical character of the Demiurge. See Cornford, *PC*, p. 38: 'He is mythical...on the other hand, he stands for a divine Reason working for ends that are good.'
[2] Even if we accept Taylor's suggestion (*Comm. on Timaeus*, p. 9) that Plato's source for the medical doctrine of the *Timaeus* was Philistion of Locri, it seems a doubtful inference that its date 'is likely to be nearer to 360 than to 347–346' and that 'probably...the *Philebus* will be later'.
[3] I quote these figures, computed by Raeder, from Cornford, *PC*, p. 13.
[4] Epistle VIII, 353 E.

his life, incorporates[1] some of the material intended for the unwritten dialogue. It is of course possible that he turned aside during these last years to write the *Philebus*; but we have left a gap of some six years (approximately 360–354) into which our dialogue may perhaps most naturally be fitted. This conjectural dating (or rather placing) which, as I would emphasise, makes no pretence to certainty, would help to account for one notable feature, namely the complete absence of political reference. Socrates and his interlocutors discuss the good for man as individual, not as member of a community; this is surprising in the author of *Republic*, *Statesman* and *Laws*, and may be taken to reflect a deliberate detachment from political speculation such as better fits the years 360–354 than any other period in Plato's last two decades. He has despaired of Dionysius, he dislikes Dion's projected recourse to arms, and he has not yet been drawn back into the Syracusan turmoil by the urgent appeal of the murdered Dion's associates.

However that may be, we can point with some assurance to a more positive reason for the composition of the *Philebus* than a temporary distaste for politics. At or about the time when Plato paid his first visit to Dionysius II there arrived in Athens the famous mathematician, astronomer and geographer Eudoxus of Cnidus. In the history of philosophy Eudoxus is chiefly of importance on account of his planetary theory, which was adopted with modifications by Aristotle; but we are here concerned only with his pronouncement, reported and discussed in the tenth book of the *Nicomachean Ethics*, that pleasure is the good. From that discussion, or rather from the whole treatment of pleasure and pain by Aristotle in the seventh and tenth books, it has been reasonably inferred that this was a much contested topic in the Platonic Academy both before and after Plato's death. That the *Philebus* influenced the discussion is obvious; what is difficult, indeed I should say impossible to determine is how many, and which, of the views reported by Aristotle had already been formulated before the *Philebus* was written. It would in particular be helpful if we knew that Speusippus had already put forward his assertion that both pleasure and pain are evils and opposed to the neutral state which is good.[2] There is no mention of this doctrine in our dialogue, and in my judgment there is no direct allusion to Speusippus to be found there; but that of course does not prove that the doctrine was unformulated,

---

[1] Especially in Book III. So Cornford, *PC*, p. 7, developing a suggestion by Raeder.   [2] *E.N.* 1153 B 5, 1173 A 6; Aulus Gellius IX, 5.

or unknown to Plato when he wrote. What does seem probable is that Speusippus's dictum, whenever it was announced, was provoked by the doctrine of Eudoxus; and that one of Plato's own motives in writing the *Philebus* was, not indeed to confute Eudoxus, but rather to restate and to some extent modify his own doctrine of pleasure and pain in the light of Eudoxus's pronouncement. At the earliest date at which our dialogue can reasonably be put, namely 360, Eudoxus had been in Athens, and in close touch with the Academy, for some seven years, and it is most unlikely that he had not by that time put forward his views about pleasure.[1]

It is however quite clear that Plato is not directly attacking Eudoxus. He might be said to attack the character called Philebus, though this would be a misleading account of a dialogue which is constructive rather than destructive, and which seeks to do justice to the rightful claim of pleasure to be a factor in human happiness. The direct refutation of Philebus's contention, that pleasure is the good (as it is expressed at the outset), or that pleasure and good are identical in nature and in meaning (as it is more definitely expressed near the end[2]), occupies only a small fraction of the discussion; the great bulk of the dialogue is devoted to the demonstration that pleasure is less valuable than intellectual activity, but that some pleasure is necessary for happiness: a demonstration which involves discriminating various kinds of pleasure, and distinguishing between true or pure pleasures and false or 'mixed'.

Hedonism is a term which may be, and has been used in various senses; but understood as the doctrine that 'pleasant' and 'good' are synonymous terms, and hence that pleasure is the 'right aim' (σκοπὸς ὀρθός) for all creatures capable of experiencing it, it had been long since refuted by Plato in the *Gorgias*. He did not want to go over the old ground again; yet he did want his readers to remember the *Gorgias* as they read the *Philebus*, and by calling the dialogue after Philebus, who takes a very small share in it, rather than after Protarchus, the chief respondent, he intends, I would suggest, to make us feel that behind the new topic—the discussion of the kinds of pleasure admissible in the good life—and conditioning that topic, there lies the old truth, so passionately proclaimed by his Socrates in a dialogue written some

---

[1] The received date of his death is circ. 355.

[2] 60 A: Φίληβός φησι τὴν ἡδονὴν σκοπὸν ὀρθὸν πᾶσι ζῴοις γεγονέναι καὶ δεῖν πάντας τούτου στοχάζεσθαι, καὶ δὴ καὶ τἀγαθὸν τοῦτ' αὐτὸ εἶναι σύμπασι, καὶ δύο ὀνόματα, ἀγαθὸν καὶ ἡδύ, ἑνί τινι καὶ φύσει μιᾷ τούτω ὀρθῶς τεθέντ' ἔχειν.

thirty years earlier, that the man who seeks pleasure indiscriminately, and confounds it with good, is untrue to his nature as a reasoning being, and degrades himself to the level of a gluttonous animal.[1]

Philebus has said his say before the dialogue opens, but he is allowed to say a few words now and then, just often enough to remind us that he is there, in other words that the ideal of Callicles lurks in the background of any talk about pleasure and pain, indeed of any talk about human life. But he does not take any real part in the discussion, for as Friedländer truly says,[2] 'Lust kann nicht Rede (Rechenschaft) geben'. Callicles could be confuted, and was, for he was willing to argue, as most people are willing to argue on matters of right and wrong, however confidently they hold their views; but Philebus is not a real person: he is the mere embodiment of an irrational dogmatic hedonism, a Callicles without the passion, the fighting spirit which makes him live in our memory, and even attracts us against our better judgment. It was, I imagine, just because Plato did not want a real man that he used a name borne, so far as we know, by no one.[3]

No contemporary reader could have imagined that Philebus stood for Eudoxus.[4] Even if we do not agree with Karpp[5] that Eudoxus's so-called hedonism was a psychological rather than an ethical doctrine (in other words, that he emphasised the fact, or apparent fact, that man like other animals aims at pleasure, but did not advance to any ethical theory as to what pleasure man, quâ rational, *ought* to pursue), in any case Philebus does not suggest the man known to his contemporaries as 'eminently moral'.[6] And, in general, it would have been a poor method of attacking Eudoxus to write a dialogue in which he was not allowed to defend his thesis himself, and in which his nominal disciple

---

[1] χαραδριοῦ τινα βίον, *Gorg.* 494 B.

[2] *Die plat. Schriften*, p. 558.

[3] Except indeed by a character in Lucian's *Asinus* (36). As this Philebus was a κίναιδος, it looks as if Lucian believed the name to be significant; he may be right: cf. the 'disclaimed innuendo' at 46 B, which suggests 'nastiness'.

[4] Prof. Taylor identifies the position of Philebus with that of Eudoxus and concludes (*Plato*, p. 410) that 'the issue discussed in the dialogue is one which had actually divided the members of the Academy, the question what is really meant by the Platonic "Form of the Good". One party thinks that it means pleasure, the other that it means thought'. I cannot understand how anyone who had read *Rep.* VI could think that the αὐτὸ ἀγαθόν meant pleasure; at the very outset of the discussion (505 c) Socrates warns us against such a supposition.

[5] H. Karpp, *Untersuchungen zur Phil. des Eudoxos*, p. 20 f.

[6] ἐπιστεύοντο δ' οἱ λόγοι διὰ τὴν τοῦ ἤθους ἀρετὴν μᾶλλον ἢ δι' αὐτούς · διαφερόντως γὰρ ἐδόκει σώφρων εἶναι· οὐ δὴ ὡς φίλος τῆς ἡδονῆς ἐδόκει ταῦτα λέγειν, ἀλλ' οὕτως ἔχειν κατ' ἀλήθειαν (*E.N.* 1172 B15). Contrast Philebus's 'mulishness' at 12 A with the reasonableness (by which I do not mean cogency) of the arguments in *Ethics* K 2.

(Protarchus) brings forward not one of the arguments which he (according to Aristotle) advanced.[1]

At this point it is convenient to notice the other two characters (apart from *personae mutae*) of the dialogue, Protarchus and Socrates. I am inclined to think that Protarchus also is an imaginary person. He has, it is true, a 'real' name,[2] and may conceivably be the same as the Protarchus whose remark is quoted by Aristotle at *Physics* 197 B 10. He is also represented as having 'heard' Gorgias (57 E), but I do not feel sure that this necessarily represents historical fact; the mention of Gorgias may be no more than an obvious device for bringing up the comparative merits of rhetoric and dialectic. In general, Protarchus seems to be just the 'ordinary listener', the average educated interlocutor needed to keep up some semblance of real discussion; not a mere dummy, for he makes, or tries to make, a point or two against Socrates, and relieves bare exposition by an occasional 'intelligent anticipation' of Socrates's points. Although he starts by donning the mantle of Philebus, his hedonism is of so eminently reasonable a type that before long he turns into a collaborator rather than an opponent of Socrates.

Surprise has sometimes been felt that Socrates should lead the conversation, when his rôle in all the other late dialogues, *Sophist*, *Statesman*, *Timaeus*, *Critias*, is quite small, and he is absent from the *Laws*. But it should be remembered that he had been cast for the questioner's part in the *Philosopher*,[3] and that there are obvious reasons why others should take the lead in the 'divisional exercises' of *Sophist* and *Statesman*, and in the physical and physiological speculations of the *Timaeus*. It is quite mistaken to suppose that 'Socrates' in our dialogue is a mere label affixed to an uncharacterised figure who might just as well have been called by any other name.[4] No doubt he is not so strongly characterised as in some of the dialogues of Plato's early and middle

---

[1] Timaeus seems to be another imaginary character, though invented for a different kind of reason; see Cornford, *PC*, pp. 2–3. He could be given a 'real' name, because there was nothing offensive in his rôle.

[2] He has also a father named Callias (19 B): but this need be no more significant than Strepsiades having a father called Pheidon, or his wife an uncle called Megacles.

[3] *Pol.* 258 A, where I follow Cornford's highly probable interpretation (*PTK*, p. 168) of Socrates's words: ἐμοὶ μὲν οὖν εἰς αὖθις, σοὶ δὲ νῦν ἀποκρινέσθω (sc. ὁ νέος Σωκράτης).

[4] So Raeder, *Platons phil. Entwickelung*, p. 354: 'Der Sokrates, der hier auftritt, hat mit dem Sokrates, der sonst in den platonischen Dialogen als Leiter des Gesprächs erscheint, nur den Namen gemeinsam.'

periods; but there are a number of passages which recall the Socrates that we know: for example, his diffidence in attaching names to the gods (12 C, cf. *Crat.* 400 D), his habit of deliberately nonplussing his hearers, as it seemed to them (20 A, cf. *Meno* 80 A), his attribution of a novel idea to something that he might have dreamt or 'heard from somebody' (20 B, cf. *Theaet.* 201 D), his bantering self-depreciation (εἰμὶ δ' ὡς ἔοικεν ἐγὼ γελοῖός τις ἄνθρωπος 23 D, cf. *Phaedrus* 236 D, *Rep.* 392 D); the semi-ironical compliment (ἀλλὰ προθύμως ἀμύνεις τῷ τῆς ἡδονῆς λόγῳ 38 A, cf. *Euthyphro* 7 A, *Theaet.* 146 D); the device of the 'dialogue within the dialogue' involving a personification of abstractions (the speeches of the pleasures and intelligences, 63 B ff.: compare the speech of the laws at *Crito* 50 A ff.). These are all distinctive traits of Plato's Socrates, though they may not all be proper to the Socrates of history.

It has been urged that in the *Philebus* Socrates is unlike himself in that he expounds rather than argues or persuades; and attention has been called to a passage (19 C) where Protarchus says: 'You made all of us a free offer of this discussion, in which you yourself were included, for the purpose of deciding what is the best of all things possessed by man.' Protarchus is here merely recalling what Socrates had arranged in the first page of the dialogue, and the word translated 'discussion' carries no necessary implication of formality, or of the relation of professor and students: it is in fact used of a Socratic conversation in such 'non-professorial' dialogues as *Laches* (201 C) and *Symposium* (176 E), as well as in *Theaetetus* (150 D) and *Sophist* (217 E). Nor do I think Socrates has become any more of an *ex cathedra* lecturer than he was already in the *Republic*; doubtless the part played by his respondents is not comparable to those of Simmias and Cebes, of Polus and Callicles, or even of Glaucon and Adimantus; but it is considerably more than that of Aristoteles, of Young Socrates, or of Megillus and Cleinias: in other words, Plato could still write a Socratic dialogue.

Nor has he forgotten or discarded what he had written in the greatest of all Socratic dialogues. If the Callicles of the *Gorgias* is to be descried behind Philebus, it is equally true that the Socrates of the *Republic* is to be descried behind Socrates. It may seem surprising that the dialogue contains no explicit account of moral virtue and its relation to happiness or the 'good life'. At the very outset it is agreed that the quest is for 'a state or condition of the soul which can render the life

of every man a happy life', and it is natural to ask what has become of
the account given in the *Republic* of 'justice' in the tripartite soul, and
of the assignment of moral virtues to its parts and their relations.

As the tripartite soul reappears in the *Timaeus*, it is not likely that
Plato has abandoned it, or its implications with regard to the nature of
moral goodness, in the *Philebus*. But he does not want to go over
familiar ground again. That no life can be happy unless reason controls
appetite, with θυμός enlisted on the side of reason, is taken for granted;
when we are told on the first page that Socrates has been contending
that 'thought, intelligence, memory, right opinion and true reasoning'
are more valuable than pleasure, we are doubtless meant to recall, and
to take as the background of all that Socrates is going to argue, the
part which he had previously shown to be played by these activities
in regulating the moral life. Moreover, the ἕξις ψυχῆς καὶ διάθεσις
which the dialogue ultimately finds in the well-mixed life is one in
which the types of pleasure admitted are welcomed by intelligence (in
the speech of the personified intelligences at 63 D–E), and include 'all
such as accompany every sort of ἀρετή', while those that attend upon
'folly and vice in general' are rejected. Plainly then Plato's conception
of moral goodness as requisite for happiness is unchanged: the welcome
given by intelligence to pleasure, and the exclusion of vicious pleasures,
implies the control of ἐπιθυμία by φρόνησις. It is only the false assumption that Plato must explicitly formulate the whole of his ethics whenever he writes on an ethical subject that might lead us astray.

Plato's range of thought is so wide, and his dialogues usually show
such a diversity of interest, that it is hazardous to pronounce that
any single idea is dominant in a particular dialogue. Nevertheless it is
perhaps permissible to pick out one conception which permeates the
Philebus, the conception namely of pleasure as an ἄπειρον, an 'unlimited' thing. It is best to leave the meaning of this unexplained in
an introduction; but if we allow it to be the dominant thought, or I
would rather say the dominant conception with which Plato works,
it will follow that the method of the dialogue is to apply Pythagorean
categories to an ethical doctrine. But at least two other ideas are
prominent. First, the procedure of classificatory division, on which he
had recently lavished so much pains in *Sophist* and *Statesman*. Division
as a master-key of science, an instrument, if not for solving, at least
for dealing with the perennial problem of the One-Many, is extolled
early in the dialogue: but its subsequent application is concealed, not

open: instead of the formal dichotomies—so immeasurably wearisome to modern readers, and, one would suppose, to ancient also—we get various kinds of pleasure and of intelligence discriminated through an informal[1] procedure, which any one who cared to do so could easily remodel into a divisional scheme. Secondly, there is the religious conviction of a Divine Mind, the cause of all that is good, rational and orderly in the universe, a νοῦς βασιλεὺς οὐρανοῦ τε καὶ γῆς (28 c): a Mind which moreover, as in the *Timaeus* and *Epinomis*, expresses itself in a mathematical ordering or determination, in fact a θεὸς ἀεὶ γεωμετρῶν.

The three ideas I have mentioned are worked into the ethical and psychological discussion with no little skill and artistry. Nobody would claim for the *Philebus* the architectural mastery displayed in the *Phaedo* and *Republic*: on the other hand the formlessness of the work has been often exaggerated. The more I have studied it, the clearer has its structure become, and the more understandable its transitions, digressions, and postponements. If any reader of this book comes to feel the same, I shall not have spent my time to no purpose.

[1] In the case of intelligence, however, the procedure approximates much more closely to formal division: but it is a much shorter treatment than that of pleasure.

TRANSLATION & COMMENTARY

11 A–12 B.   *Statement of the issue. The Good for Man*

The opening paragraphs give the situation presupposed by the dialogue. Philebus has asserted the view that pleasure is the good for all living creatures. Some further light is thrown on this at 60 A, where it is said that he maintains that pleasure is the *right aim* for all living things, and that they all *ought* to seek it: that they all do in fact seek it he does not appear to assert; hence his position is not precisely that of Eudoxus (Aristotle, *E.N.* 1172 B9), who did maintain this. The later passage further tells us that Philebus held 'good' and 'pleasant' to be identical in meaning: his Hedonism is therefore of an extreme type, which allows no value to anything except pleasure. Socrates's 'Intellectualism' on the other hand is not extreme: intelligence, thought, and the like are better than pleasure for all beings capable of them: a thesis which does not exclude an intrinsic value of pleasure.

Socrates has claimed superior value for intellectual activities in general, and here names several, including τὸ φρονεῖν and δόξα ὀρθή. Throughout most of the dialogue φρόνησις will be the counterpart of ἡδονή, and will be used in a wide, vague sense, not to be made precise until we come to the classification of forms of knowledge or intelligence at 55 C. Meanwhile the main distinction probably intended, or at all events that which would at once spring to the mind of readers familiar with the *Meno* and *Republic*, is that between knowledge, properly so called, and right opinion: the latter, they would remember, is of value as being the highest form of cognition of which the unphilosophic majority of mankind is capable.

There is nothing to suggest that Socrates has referred to any metaphysical or supersensible Good, or discussed the 'Form of the Good'. Both parties have however been concerned with something wider than the good for Man; but it is this that Plato is to make the subject of his dialogue; hence Socrates now makes the suggestion, which Protarchus readily accepts, that the quest shall be for a condition of soul capable of providing human happiness. This initial agreement is natural enough; but we may observe that it rules out the possibility that our good may consist in external possessions, such as wealth or the esteem of our fellows (πλοῦτος or τιμή), which Aristotle (*E.N.* 1095 A23) mentions along with pleasure as being commonly deemed to constitute happiness. Hedonism and Socraticism have this much in common, that they both find the human good within ourselves.

It is suggested that neither pleasure nor intelligence, but some third thing, may be what we seek; this will later be confirmed. Protarchus is willing to allow the possibility, but Philebus remains opposed to all compromise: 'I think, and shall continue to think, that Pleasure is victorious, whatever happens.'

Socrates   *Protarchus*   *Philebus*

Soc. Now, Protarchus, consider what the two theories are: the one 11 A
which you mean now to take over from Philebus, and the other which
I and my friends maintain, and which you are to dispute if you don't
find it to your liking. Would you like us to summarise them both?   B
Pro. Yes, do.
Soc. Well, Philebus says that the good[1] for all animate beings
consists in enjoyment, pleasure, delight, and whatever can be classed
as consonant therewith: whereas our contention is that the good is not
that, but that thought, intelligence, memory and things akin to these,
right opinion and true reasoning, prove better and more valuable than
pleasure for all such beings as can participate in them; and that for all
these, whether now living or yet to be born, nothing in the world is
more profitable than so to participate. That, I think, Philebus, is the
substance of our respective theories, is it not?
Phil. Yes, Socrates, that is perfectly correct.
Soc. Well, Protarchus, will you take over this argument now offered
to you?
Prot. I must: our fair friend Philebus has cried off.
Soc. Then ought we to do everything we can to get at the truth of
the matter?
Prot. Indeed we ought.   D
Soc. Well then, I want us to reach agreement on one further point.
Prot. What is that?
Soc. What you and I are now to attempt is to put forward a certain
state or condition of the soul which can render the life of every man a
happy life.[2] Am I right?
Prot. Quite right.

[1] I agree with Dr Bury's additional note (p. 215) that ἀγαθόν here = τὸ ἀγαθόν.
Philebus's contention is more clearly and fully expressed at 60 A.
[2] From the wording here it might be supposed that Plato intends a distinction
between the disposition of soul that brings, or is a means to, happiness, and
happiness itself. But no such distinction is maintained in the sequel: the Mixed
Life of intelligence and some kinds of pleasure, which proves to be the human
good, is conceived not merely as a ἕξις or διάθεσις ψυχῆς but as an ἐνέργεια also;
that is to say, Plato feels it natural to assume that a good ἕξις will exhibit itself
in good activities. Aristotle, in insisting (*E.N.* 1098 B 31 ff.) that happiness must
be an ἐνέργεια, not a mere ἕξις, may be thinking of our present passage, though
probably he has more directly in mind Speusippus, who τὴν εὐδαιμονίαν φησὶν ἕξιν
εἶναι τελείαν ἐν τοῖς κατὰ φύσιν ἔχουσιν, ἢ ἕξιν ἀγαθῶν (Ritter and Preller, *Hist. Phil.
Graec.* § 356). In any case his criticism holds rather against the letter than the
spirit of the Academic view.

Soc. Then you people put forward the state of enjoyment, whereas we put forward that of intelligence?

Prot. Yes.

E *Soc.* But suppose some other state better than these be found: then, if it were found more akin to pleasure, I imagine that while we both of us yield to the life that securely possesses the features in question, the 12A life of pleasure overcomes that of intelligence.

Prot. Yes.

Soc. But if it were found more akin to intelligence, then intelligence is victorious over pleasure, and it is pleasure that is worsted. What do you two say? Is that agreed?

Prot. I think so, for my part.

Soc. And you, Philebus? What do you say?

Phil. What I think, and shall continue to think, is that pleasure is victorious whatever happens. But you must decide for yourself, Protarchus.

Prot. Now that you have handed over the argument to us, Philebus, you are no longer in a position to agree with Socrates or to disagree.

B *Phil.* True; but no matter: I wash my hands of the affair, and hereby call the goddess herself to witness that I do so.

Prot. You can have ourselves too as additional witnesses to one point, namely that you have said what you have. And now, Socrates, we must attempt (and Philebus may choose to help us or do as he likes) to come to a conclusion on what comes next.

Soc. Yes, we must make the attempt: and plainly we shall begin with the goddess herself, who, according to our friend, is called Aphrodite, though her truest name, he tells us, is Pleasure.

Prot. Excellent.

12 B–13 D *Pleasure as a generic unity, containing a variety of species*

Philebus has sought to buttress his position by an identification of Pleasure with Aphrodite. Socrates, whose deep religious sense always mistrusts the tales of mythology and even the names given to gods and goddesses—since these may be unacceptable to them as implying a falsification of their real nature (cf. *Crat.* 400 D)—points out the great variety of pleasures; a fact which, as Plato intends us to see, at once rules out Philebus's identification: a god is of simple or single nature (ἁπλοῦς, *Rep.* 380 D) not ποικίλος.[1]

Protarchus at first contends that though the sources of our pleasures may be different, and even opposite to one another, the actual pleasant

---

[1] Contrast 12 C μορφὰς δὲ δήπου παντοίας εἴληφε (sc. ἡδονή) with *Rep.* 381 B ἥκιστα ἂν πολλὰς μορφὰς ἴσχοι ὁ θεός.

feeling is always the same. This is at bottom a question for psychology to pronounce upon; Socrates does not here attempt a psychological examination, but insists that Protarchus' ground for asserting this is really *logical*—or rather *illogical*, inasmuch as he takes no account of the difference between generic and specific identity. Socrates's parallel of the generic term 'colour' forces Protarchus to give ground for a moment, but when Socrates goes on to point out that the generic identity of all pleasure is compatible with the existence of some good, and some bad pleasures, he reverts to his previous position, that the difference does not lie within the pleasures themselves. Socrates protests against the futility of such barren logomachy, parrying his opponent by the quip that it might equally well be maintained that 'the completely unlike is completely like the completely unlike' (τὸ ἀνο-μοιότατόν ἐστι τῷ ἀνομοιοτάτῳ πάντων ὁμοιότατον). They must, he suggests, start a new approach, and get properly to grips. The logomachy is to be got rid of in the next section.

Socrates   Protarchus

Soc. For myself, Protarchus, in the matter of naming the gods I am 12 C always more fearful than you would think a man could be: nothing indeed makes me so afraid. So in this case I call Aphrodite by any name that is pleasing to her; but as for pleasure, I know that it is a thing of variety and, as I said, it is with pleasure that we must start, turning our thoughts to an examination of its nature. Of course the mere word 'pleasure' suggests a unity, but surely the forms it assumes are of all sorts and, in a sense, unlike each other. For example, we say that an immoral man feels pleasure, and that a moral man feels it too just in being moral: again, we say the same of a fool whose mind is a D mass of foolish opinions and hopes: or once again an intelligent man, we say, is pleased just by being intelligent;[1] now if anyone asserts that these several kinds of pleasure are like each other, surely he will deserve to be thought foolish?

Prot. They are unlike, because they arise from opposite sources, Socrates: nevertheless in themselves they are not opposites. How could pleasure be opposite to pleasure?[2] Surely nothing in the world E could be more completely similar than a thing to itself.

---

[1] The general scheme of the dialogue proceeds on the basis of the contemporary antithesis of intelligence and pleasure; but Plato is well aware that the highest kind of pleasure transcends the antithesis, and the pleasures of learning will be explicitly recognised at 52 A.

[2] I retain μή, and place a question-mark after ἡδονή, following an unpublished suggestion of the late Prof. Henry Jackson. μή = *num*, and οὐχ goes closely with ὁμοιότατον: 'surely it could not be other than most similar'.

Soc. As, of course, colour to colour. What a man you are! Certainly, in respect simply of its all being colour there will be no difference, but for all that everyone recognises that black is not merely different from white, but in fact its absolute opposite.[1] Then again the same applies as between figure and figure; taken as a class all figure is one, but of 13 A its divisions some are absolutely opposite to each other, while others have countless points of difference: and we can find many other instances of the same thing. So you mustn't put any faith in this argument that makes all sorts of absolutely opposite things into one thing. I am afraid we are going to find pleasures in some cases opposite to pleasures.

Prot. Maybe: but what harm will that do to the argument of our side?

Soc. This, that though the things in question are unlike you designate them by a name other than their own: that is what we shall reply. You say, I mean, that all pleasant things are good. Now of course nobody attempts to maintain the thesis that pleasant things B are not pleasant; but though they are in some cases (indeed in most) bad and in others good—so those who think with me maintain— nevertheless you designate them all as good, although you would agree that they are unlike if anyone were to press you in argument.[2] What then is the identical element present alike[3] in the bad pleasures and in the good that makes you use the term 'good' in reference to them all?

Prot. What do you mean, Socrates? Do you imagine that anyone will agree, after maintaining that pleasure is the good—that having

---

[1] Socrates's analogy is not really cogent, for Protarchus might have replied that there is no counterpart in 'pleasure', if taken in his own sense, viz. as pleasant feeling *per se*, to the distinction of black and white in colour; but that such a distinction can only arise if 'pleasure' is taken in the other sense, viz. the complex of feeling and source of feeling. It is, in fact, this second sense which is implied in all Socrates's argument in the present section.

We have here one of many instances in the dialogues in which Plato allows a fallacy to be committed by one of his characters—deliberately allows it, since he could not have written 12 D7–E2 without a clear consciousness of the two senses of 'pleasure'. Why does he do this? I think we must answer, because he believed that there are qualitative differences between mere pleasure-feelings (that e.g. the feeling aroused by hearing great music is qualitatively different from that aroused by eating sweets), in other words that ἡδονή, τοῦτο αὐτό (as Protarchus phrases it), is a genus of species, yet he could not prove it. He may also have considered that it was unreasonable to expect him to prove it, since the isolated pleasure-feeling is a mere abstraction: what really occurs is always 'my pleasure in this', an indivisible whole though divisible in analysis.

[2] Socrates's point is that generic identity can never of itself justify the attribution to the species of a genus, still less to their particulars, of any common quality other than that denoted by the generic term.

[3] For a defence of ἐνόν in B 4 see Burnet in *C.Q.* xv, p. 1.

done that he will endure to be told by you that certain pleasures are c good, and certain others bad?

Soc. Well, at all events you will allow that they are unlike, and in some cases opposite to, each other.

Prot. Not in so far as they are just pleasures.

Soc. We are drifting back to the old position, Protarchus; it seems that we are not going to allow even that one pleasure differs from another, all being alike: the examples given just now cause us no compunction: our beliefs and assertions will be those of the most commonplace persons, and most puerile in discussion. D

Prot. What exactly are you referring to?

Soc. I mean this: supposing that I were to retort by copying your method and were brazen enough to maintain that a pair of completely dissimilar things are completely similar,[1] then I could say just what you say, with the result that we should be shown up as extraordinarily puerile, and our discussion would 'stranded be and perish'. Let us get it back again, then, into the water: then I daresay we shall be able to get fairly to grips and possibly come to agreement with each other.

Prot. Tell me how, will you? E

Soc. You must be the questioner this time, Protarchus, and I will answer.

Prot. What question precisely?

13 E–15 C   *The Problem of the One and the Many*

By admitting that knowledge is, equally with pleasure, a merely generic unity, Socrates induces Protarchus to concede the specific variety of pleasures. But the discussion does not proceed forthwith to a classification of pleasures and forms of knowledge. Behind the immediate question, which has been *practically* settled in the sense that both parties are agreed on the need for classification, lies the general problem, how classification can be logically justified: in other words, how one thing can be also many things.

In one or another of its forms, this problem is co-extensive with the history of Greek philosophy. It is the central theme of the *Parmenides*, and a prominent issue in the *Sophist*. In the hands of Plato's contemporary Antisthenes it had given rise to a peculiar theory of predication, reported by Aristotle[2] and probably alluded to by Plato in the *Theaetetus*.[3]

---

[1] Each opposite, being called τὸ ἀνομοιότατον, must be ὁμοιότατον to the other.

[2] *Met.* 1024 B 32 Ἀντισθένης ᾤετο εὐήθως μηθὲν ἀξιῶν λέγεσθαι πλὴν τῷ οἰκείῳ λόγῳ ἐν ἐφ' ἑνός.

[3] 201 Dff. See Cornford, *PTK*, pp. 143–4; *Plato and Parmenides*, pp. 72–4.

The crudest form of the problem, namely the attribution of a number of predicates to a single concrete subject (e.g. 'Socrates is short, old and ugly'), is dismissed as trivial both here and in the *Parmenides* and *Sophist*. There is no reason why Socrates should not 'partake' of any number of Forms simultaneously, even if (as here, 14 D) the Forms be contraries like Greatness and Smallness, Heaviness and Lightness. Nor need any difficulty be felt in respect of the unity which a concrete particular combines with the plurality of its parts. To exploit the problem in these forms is merely eristic. The real problem concerns the unity-in-plurality of the Forms themselves: how can these Unities retain their unity while split up, as the Theory of Forms seems to require, amongst an indefinite number of particulars?

Socrates   Protarchus

13 E   *Soc.* When I was asked originally what the good[1] is, I suggested intelligence, knowledge, mind, and so on, as being good: now won't they be in the same case with your own suggestion?

Prot. Will they? Why?

Soc. Knowledge taken in its entirety will seem to be a plurality in which this knowledge is unlike that—even, it may be, this knowledge opposite to that: but, if it were, should I be a fit person to carry on

14 this present discussion if I took alarm at the point in question and maintained that knowledge is never unlike knowledge, thereby bringing our discussion to an end like a tale that is told, while we ourselves escaped from the wreck on a quibble?

Prot. Well, of course, we've got to escape, but it mustn't be like that. However, I am attracted by having your thesis on all fours with my own. Let us take it that there are this plurality and unlikeness, or difference, in pleasure as in knowledge.

B   *Soc.* Well then, Protarchus, don't let us shut our eyes to the variety that attaches to your good[2] as to mine: let us have the varieties fairly before us and make a bold venture in the hope that perhaps they may, on inspection, reveal whether we ought to give the title of the Good to pleasure or to intelligence or to some third thing. For I imagine we are not striving merely to secure a victory for my suggestions or for yours: rather we ought both of us to fight in support of the truth and the whole truth.

---

[1] Here, as at 11 B, ἀγαθόν must mean 'the good': but Socrates had answered the question by saying what was good, in the sense of being better, at all events, than pleasure (τῆς γε ἡδονῆς ἀμείνω καὶ λῷω).

[2] I retain τοῦ ἀγαθοῦ in B 1 and adopt Stallbaum's ἐλεγχόμεναι in B 3.

Prot. We ought indeed.[1]

Soc. Then let us come to an agreement that will give us a still surer c basis for this assertion.

Prot. To what assertion do you refer?

Soc. The one that causes everybody trouble, whether they want it to, as some people sometimes do, or not, as others sometimes do not.

Prot. I wish you would be plainer.

Soc. I am referring to the assertion which came our way just now, and which is of a truly remarkable character. For really it is a remarkable thing to say that many are one, and one is many; a person who suggests either of these things may well encounter opposition.

Prot. Do you mean a person who says that I, Protarchus, though I am one human being am nevertheless many Protarchuses of opposite D kinds, making me out to be both tall and short, both heavy and light, and so on and so forth, though I am really always the same person?

Soc. That isn't what I mean, Protarchus: the remarkable instances of one-and-many that you have mentioned are commonplace: almost everyone agrees nowadays that there is no need to concern oneself with things like that, feeling that they are childish, obvious and a great nuisance to argument; for that matter, the same applies to another class of instances, in which you discriminate a man's several limbs and mem- E bers, get your opponent to admit that the individual in question is all those limbs and members, and then make him look ridiculous by showing that he has been compelled to make the incredible assertions that the one is many and indeed infinitely many, and that the many are only one.

Prot. Then if these are commonplace instances, Socrates, and everyone agrees about them, what are the other sort that you speak of involving this same assertion?

Soc. The One that is taken, my dear boy, may be something that 15 comes into being and perishes, as it was in the cases we have just been speaking of; with such cases, with a One like that, it is admitted, as we said a moment ago, that there is no need to thrash the matter out. But suppose you venture to take as your One such things as Man, Ox, the Beautiful, the Good, then you have the sort of unities that involve you in dispute if you give them your serious attention and subject them to division.[2]

---

[1] Thus Protarchus, almost at the outset, is distinguished, as a person with whom Socrates can argue, from Philebus with whom he cannot (12 A).

[2] The text has been doubted, but is probably sound. It is equivalent to τὸ πολλὰ περὶ τούτων διαιρουμένους σπουδάζειν ἀμφισβήτησις (= matter of dispute) γίγνεται.

Prot. What sort of dispute?

B   *Soc.* First, whether we ought to believe in the real existence of monads of this sort; secondly, how we are to conceive that each of them, being always one and the same and subject neither to generation nor destruction, nevertheless is, to begin with, most assuredly this single unity and yet subsequently comes to be in the infinite number of things that come into being—an identical unity being thus found simultaneously in unity and in plurality. Is it torn in pieces, or does the whole of it (and this would seem the extreme of impossibility) get
C apart from itself?[1] It is not your questions, Protarchus, but these questions, where the One and Many are of another kind, that cause all manner of dissatisfaction if they are not properly settled, and satisfaction if they are.

Prot. Then there, Socrates, is the first task for us to achieve here and now.

Soc. That is what I should say.

Prot. Well then, you may regard all of us here as agreeing with you herein. As for Philebus, perhaps we had better not put him any more questions at present, but let the sleeping dog lie.

15 D–17 A   *Dialectic in relation to the One-Many problem*

That One should be Many and Many One must always remain a paradox, yet it will become less of an impediment to thought if, rather than seeking to exploit it polemically in the current fashion, we apply a 'dialectical' treatment to it. Instead of setting up an unmediated antithesis, we must try to see—taking a hint from the Limit and Unlimited of Pythagoreanism—how each generic unity contains within itself a definite number of 'kinds' mediating between itself and the infinity of particulars into which it ultimately vanishes. There are

---

[1] Scholars have differed as to whether there are two questions here or three. I believe there are only two: (1) do the monads really exist? (2) how can these eternal and immutable beings *come to be* in a plurality of particulars? Archer-Hind (*J. of Ph.* xxvii, pp. 229 ff.) and Friedländer (*Die plat. Schr.* p. 567) think that the second question is put in the words εἶτα πῶς...μίαν ταύτην, and concerns the systematic unity of the Forms themselves, i.e. how do they combine into a unity? But on this interpretation I cannot see any relevance in μήτε γένεσιν μήτε ὄλεθρον προσδεχομένην, a phrase which seems clearly to bear on a Form's immanence in particulars (ἐν τοῖς γιγνομένοις...πολλὰ γεγονυῖαν), nor any meaning in the word ταύτην. I have adopted the best suggestion known to me, that of J. B. Bury, as reported in R. G. Bury's edition, p. 216: viz. to read ὅμως εἶναι βεβαιότατα α (=πρῶτον) μὲν ταύτην (the μίαν might perhaps be retained after μέν, though it could be dispensed with), μετὰ δὲ τοῦτ' κτλ. Thus μετὰ δὲ τοῦτο will not belong to the series πρῶτον μέν, εἶτα etc., but will answer the second πρῶτον μέν. This gives a clumsy, but not impossible sentence.

many 'Ones' between our original One and our original Many, and the task of the philosopher is to see what these intermediates are, and how many they are.

The method, of which Socrates says he has always been an admirer, is that of Division (διαίρεσις), which makes its first clear appearance in the *Phaedrus*, and is abundantly illustrated in the *Sophist* and *Statesman*, where it is applied to the purpose of defining a species: but as Prof. Cornford points out (*Plato's Theory of Knowledge*, p. 171), the method may be used also for 'the classification of all the species falling under a genus in a complete table'. It is this use that Socrates is now describing, and he lays special emphasis on the *objective* character of the classification—the classes must not be too many nor too few: the right number, which the philosopher aims at finding, corresponds to the Forms really existing, not to arbitrary 'kinds' made by ourselves: that is why dialectical method is 'quite easy to indicate, but very far from easy to employ'.

Plato, in characteristic fashion, here professes to find the origin of his own dialectical method in a doctrine of 'a Prometheus', that is to say Pythagoras, whose discovery that Limit and the Unlimited are the principles of all things is thus put on a level with the discovery of fire. We are not, of course, to suppose that Pythagoras himself or his school concerned themselves with scientific classification, or addressed themselves to the logical problem here under discussion. Yet inasmuch as that classification is a counterpart of the real world of Forms, the logical problem is merged in the ontological, and Plato means us to understand that the Pythagoreans' endeavour to penetrate to the principle of Limit, which orders and 'informs' the unintelligible 'chaos' of the Unlimited, is essentially one with his own endeavour to trace the formal structure of the world that underlies, and gives its reality and meaning to, the world of sense experience. We shall find the metaphysical significance, rather than the logical, of πέρας and ἄπειρον discussed in a later section (23 c ff.).

In referring to the Pythagorean principles, Socrates mentions One and Many first, Limit and Unlimitedness second. The order is dictated no doubt by the preceding context: the antithesis ἓν-πλῆθος does figure amongst the ten pairs of Pythagorean opposites (Ar. *Met.* 986 A 24), but it seems clear that it was a secondary, or rather a tertiary, antithesis— an application of the primary pair πέρας and ἄπειρον: the second pair in Aristotle's list is Odd-Even. For an illuminating discussion of these Pythagorean principles the reader may be referred to F. M. Cornford, *Plato and Parmenides*, pp. 1–27.

Socrates   Protarchus

Soc. Very well. Now what is to be our first move in the great 15 D battle of all arms that rages on this issue? Here's a suggestion.

Prot. Yes?

Soc. We'll put the thing like this: we get this identity of the one and the many cropping up everywhere as the result of the sentences we utter;[1] in every single sentence ever uttered, in the past and in the present, there it is. What we are dealing with is a problem that will assuredly never cease to exist; this is not its first appearance; rather it is, in my view, something incidental to sentences themselves, never to pass, never to fade. As soon as a young man gets wind of it, he is as E delighted as if he had discovered an intellectual gold-mine; he is beside himself with delight, and loves to try every move in the game; first he rolls the stuff to one side and jumbles it into one, then he undoes it again and takes it to pieces, to the confusion first and foremost of himself, next of his neighbours at the moment, whether they be younger or older or of his own age: he has no mercy on his father or mother 16 or anyone else listening to him; a little more, and he would victimise even animals, as well as human beings in general, including foreigners, to whom of course he would never show mercy provided he could get hold of an interpreter.

Prot. Let me call your attention, Socrates, to the fact that there are plenty of us here, all young people: aren't you afraid that we shall join with Philebus in an assault on you, if you keep abusing us? Well, well, we realise what you mean: perhaps there is some way, some device

---

[1] The words ταὐτὸν ἕν καὶ πολλὰ ὑπὸ λόγων γιγνόμενα (where ταὐτόν should be taken as predicate of γιγνόμενα) are not, I think, intended to imply that the paradox is unreal inasmuch as language is untrue to reality. Every 'sentence' (by which is meant every subject-predicate proposition) exhibits this paradoxical identity, since the Form-predicate is 'participated' by the subject, and it must be acknowledged as truly paradoxical. What matters, however, is that it should not be exploited eristically, but mitigated, rendered tolerable, by the dialectic procedure now to be described.

If it be asked whether the problems of 15 B are here solved, as 15 C has led us to expect, we must reply that they are not; nor indeed could they be solved so long as Universals (Forms, Ideas) were regarded as existents belonging to a higher order of Being than particulars, existents in such a sense that each Form itself *has* the character that it *is* (as e.g. at *Parm.* 132 A αὐτὸ τὸ μέγα is thought of as *having* the character of Greatness, or at *Prot.* 330 D αὐτὴ ἡ ὁσιότης as *having* that of Holiness). There is no clear evidence that Plato ever ceased to think of Forms as 'existent' in this sense: he certainly does so think of them here, for if he did not the problems would not arise.

But if the difficulty of μέθεξις (i.e. of reconciling the Form's unity with its μετέχεσθαι) is not solved, here or elsewhere, it may fairly be said to be 'properly settled' and 'made a cause of satisfaction', as promised at 15 C. What we must do is to understand *how* each One is also many, and *how many* it is, not in the sense of solving a logical or metaphysical puzzle, but in the sense of discovering the real 'articulation' of each One (genus or species) down to the point at which it vanishes into the unknowable multiplicity of particulars. This is what matters for science, for the philosopher.

for getting this bothersome business to oblige us by removing itself
from our discussion, and we might discover some more attractive B
method of approach to the subject; if so, pray do your best about it,
and we will keep you company; to the best of our power, that is, for
we have a big subject in front of us, Socrates.

Soc. Big indeed, my boys, if I may adopt Philebus's style of
addressing you. Nevertheless there is not, and cannot be, a more
attractive method than that to which I have always been devoted,
though often in the past it has eluded me so that I was left desolate and
helpless.

Prot. Do tell us what it is.

Soc. It is a method quite easy to indicate, but very far from easy to C
employ. It is indeed the instrument through which every discovery
ever made in the sphere of the arts and sciences has been brought to
light. Let me describe it for your consideration.

Prot.. Please do.

Soc. There is a gift of the gods—so at least it seems evident to me—
which they let fall from their abode; and it was through Prometheus,
or one like him, that it reached mankind, together with a fire exceeding
bright. The men of old, who were better than ourselves and dwelt
nearer the gods, passed on this gift in the form of a saying: all things
(so it ran) that are ever said to be consist of a one and a many, and have
in their nature a conjunction of Limit and Unlimitedness. This then D
being the ordering of things we ought, they said, whatever it be that
we are dealing with, to assume a single form and search for it, for we
shall find it there contained; then, if we have laid hold of that, we must
go on from one form to look for two, if the case admits of there being
two,[1] otherwise for three or some other number of forms: and we must
do the same again with each of the 'ones' thus reached, until we come
to see not merely that the one that we started with is a one and an
unlimited many,[2] but also just how many it is. But we are not to apply
the character of unlimitedness to our plurality until we have discerned
the total number of forms the thing in question has intermediate

---

[1] That dichotomy is not always possible is recognised at *Pol.* 287 C: κατὰ μέλη
τοίνυν αὐτὰς (sc. τὰς τέχνας) οἷον ἱερεῖον διαιρῶμεν ἐπειδὴ δίχα ἀδυνατοῦμεν. δεῖ γὰρ εἰς
τὸν ἐγγύτατα ὅτι μάλιστα τέμνειν ἀριθμὸν ἀεί.

[2] The words πολλά and ἄπειρα do not, I think, refer to species (μέσα) and
particulars respectively, as some have supposed; rather they both refer to the
plural element or pluralised aspect of any genus, that is to species and particulars
undiscriminated; just as they do at 14 E, where the conception of 'intermediates'
(μέσα) is plainly not yet present.

E between its One and its unlimited number: it is only then, when we have done that, that we may let each one of all these intermediate forms pass away into the unlimited and cease bothering about them.[1] There then; that is how the gods, as I told you, have committed to us the task of
17 enquiry, of learning, and of teaching one another; but your clever modern man, while making his One (or his Many, as the case may be) more quickly or more slowly than is proper,[2] when he has got his One proceeds to his unlimited number straight away, allowing the intermediates to escape him; whereas it is the recognition of those intermediates that makes all the difference between a philosophical and a contentious discussion.

17 A–18 D   *Illustrations of Limit and Unlimited*

Three illustrations are now given of the method above described. The first two—sound in speech and musical sound—show the mediated passage from a One to an indefinite plurality; the third—the letters of the alphabet—is said to illustrate the reverse procedure.

(1) The first example is straightforward. Between 'sound' or 'utterance' as a genus and the infinity of particular sounds we must interpose the species, vowels, sonants and mutes, though Socrates reserves the mention of these until the third illustration. Further, the species 'vowel' includes (in the English alphabet) A E I O U, each of which is a narrower species, and the same applies to 'sonant' and 'mute'. Below these comes the infinity of particular letters used in speech.

(2) In the example of musical sound the procedure is different. The terms 'high', 'low' and 'level' are not the names of species of sound,

---

[1] There is a certain ambiguity in the use of the terms ἀπειρία and τὸ ἄπειρον running through this passage, due chiefly to the somewhat unreal suggestion that Platonic dialectic is an application of Pythagorean principles. Primarily they denote infinite plurality (that which is ἄπειρον πλήθει), but since the infinite multitude of individuals may be thought of as a multitude which cannot be known or defined because of their 'particularity', there is a secondary meaning 'indefinite', 'devoid of Form or Limit'. It is in this secondary sense that we are told not to 'apply the character of unlimitedness to our plurality' until we have reached the extreme point at which Limit ceases to be applicable, i.e. until we reach the *infimae species*.

[2] The clause ἓν μέν...τοῦ δέοντος is difficult to interpret, but the text seems defensible. It must refer to something in the Eristic's procedure other than the 'leap' from One to infinite plurality spoken of in the δέ clause, and in view of what is said at A 3–5 it probably marks a less important defect of his procedure. The meaning may be that whether he is quick or slow in demonstrating, to his interlocutor's satisfaction (or chagrin), that πολλά (i.e. ἄπειρα) are ἕν, or conversely that ἕν is ἄπειρα πλήθει, he will in either case not spend the due time, that namely which the dialectician will spend in setting out the μέσα and reaching the *infimae species*. I have discussed this passage in *C.Q.* January 1939.

which can be further divided into sub-species: nor is sound here thought of as a genus. Sound, in the musical sense, is the name of a *continuum*, a range of pitch, and 'high' and 'low' denote indefinite portions of this range stretching from any point taken in it, the point itself being the ὁμότονον, the 'level' pitch which is neither high nor low. The *continuum* can be regarded either as a unity, or as an indefinite plurality of sounds; but musical science mediates this opposition by marking off certain intervals below and above the ὁμότονον in such a way as to produce scales (ἁρμονίαι), in which each note which bounds an interval is determinately and numerically related to every other. Limit is thus imposed on the Unlimited, Form on the Formless; the One-Many has become that One that is *just so many* as the laws of concord permit. Corresponding to the measured scales are the measured movements and rhythms of those who dance to music.

It will be realised that this second example, although it illustrates one kind of rational treatment of the One-Many problem, does not illustrate dialectic, and is of no direct relevance to that classification of pleasures and kinds of knowledge from which the present digression took its departure. Plato however wants his readers to see that the Limit and Unlimited are not merely logical notions: and the musical illustration is all the more natural in that the Pythagoreans themselves conceived πέρας and ἄπειρον in this application, probably from the time of the Master himself.

No doubt Plato sees an affinity between the musical scales and the real kinds or species discovered by Division. They are not, in his view, dependent on our taste or aesthetic sense: they are just as objectively existent as the real kinds into which Nature falls, and it is for us to discover them.

(3) The third illustration is somewhat difficult to grasp, because the pre-alphabetical condition of language assumed by the legend of Theuth needs an effort of imagination. We are to suppose that mankind emitted the same vocal sounds as they still do, without having any names for them and without recognising any clear differences between them. The first stage of the nascent 'art of letters' was to discriminate what we now call vowels, continuants[1] and mutes as kinds of sound: then under each kind narrower kinds (e.g. in the case of mutes B K T etc.) would be recognised as coming; and the final step was to give these narrower kinds the common name στοιχεῖον ('element' of language, letter), that common name constituting a bond of unity (δεσμός) enabling men to conceive all the *particular* letters which they used, the indefinitely numerous B's, K's, T's, etc., as a mediated One-Many of speech.

Plato evidently regards this procedure as the reverse of the method of Division: instead of working down from a μία ἰδέα (genus) through species and sub-species to the ἀπειρία of particulars, we are supposed

---

[1] These include spirants, liquids, and nasals.

(18 A9—B3) to work upwards from particulars through sub-species and species to a genus. Yet the 'method of Theuth' cannot in fact be so regarded. In the first place, instead of being at each stage a process of grouping or sorting of a Many under an intermediate One, it involves a process of Division (διῄρει, 18 C3): and secondly, although we are apparently meant to regard 'Letter' (στοιχεῖον) as the genus finally reached, it is plain that what Theuth has done is merely to give a name to a generic notion which must have been present to his mind from the outset. The truth is that you cannot arrange objects in co-ordinate kinds or groups without thinking of these as kinds or groups *of* a 'One', i.e. into which a 'One' falls.

In short, Plato's notion that a One-Many can be dealt with by science in two alternative ways is incorrect; you must start with the conjoint apprehension of a Genus and an indefinite Many, and proceed by division until you reach *infimae species*, where your task ends. Plato evidently saw this when he described the method of dialectic in general terms at 16 C: and the *Sophist* and *Statesman* have nothing to say of a reverse procedure. Unfortunately his attempts to illustrate the method are more confusing than helpful: the first illustration is, indeed, a real one if we supplement its very brief statement by taking account of the details of the third; but the third itself is confused, and the second, as we have seen, is not in fact an illustration of dialectic at all.

It might perhaps be thought that in the 'Theuth' procedure Plato is describing the method of 'Collection' (συναγωγή) announced in the *Phaedrus* (265 D) as the complement, or rather the requisite preliminary, of Division. But this method is applicable only when we are seeking the definition of a species, not when our aim is the classification of all the species that fall under one genus. Even when definition of a species is sought, as in *Sophist* and *Statesman*, Collection is usually omitted: of the seven attempts to define the Sophist only one has its Division preceded by a Collection, namely the sixth (226 A ff.), where the 'Art of Separating' (διακριτική) is 'collected' out of the subordinate arts of filtering, sifting, winnowing etc. It would appear that Plato came to attach less importance to συναγωγή than he does in the formal first announcement of it in the *Phaedrus*. It is, moreover, in any case a method which takes no account of particulars, but only of species; and for that reason alone it cannot be what Plato attempts to formulate here as the reverse of the 'descent' from ἕν to ἄπειρα πλήθει.

Protarchus   Socrates   Philebus

17A   Prot. I think I understand, more or less, part of what you say, Socrates, but there are some points I want to get further cleared up.

Soc. My meaning, Protarchus, is surely clear in the case of the
B alphabet: so take the letters of your school-days as illustrating it.

Prot. How do you mean?

Soc. The sound that proceeds through our mouths, yours and mine and everybody's, is one, isn't it, and also an unlimited variety?

Prot. To be sure.

Soc. And we have no real understanding if we stop short at knowing it either simply as an unlimited variety, or simply as one. What makes a man 'lettered' is knowing the number and the kinds of sounds.

Prot. Very true.

Soc. Then again, it is just the same sort of thing that makes a man musical.

Prot. How so?

Soc. If you take the art of music, don't you get, as before, a sound c that is one?

Prot. Of course.

Soc. And may we put down a distinction between low, high, and the level¹ in pitch?

Prot. That's right.

Soc. But you wouldn't be a person of real understanding in music if you knew no more than these three terms, though indeed if you didn't know them you'd be of practically no account in musical matters.

Prot. I should indeed.

Soc. But when you have grasped, my dear friend, the number and nature of the intervals formed by high-pitch and low-pitch in sound, and the notes that bound those intervals, and all the systems of notes D that result from them, the systems which we have learnt, conformably to the teaching of the men of old days who discerned them, to call 'scales': and when, further, you have grasped certain corresponding features of the performer's bodily movements, features that must, so we are told, be numerically determined and be called 'figures' and 'measures', bearing in mind all the time that this is always the right way to deal with the one-and-many problem: only then, when you have grasped all this, have you gained real understanding; and whatever E be the 'one' that you have selected for investigating, that is the way to get insight about it. On the other hand, the unlimited variety that belongs to and is inherent in the particulars leaves one, in each particular case, an unlimited ignoramus, a person of no account, a veritable back

¹ ὁμότονον appears to mean a sound which is 'on a level' of pitch with the speaking voice, and so not felt as either high or low. It corresponds to 'middle C' on the pianoforte, though it need not be restricted to a single note, but may cover a certain limited stretch of notes.

number because he hasn't ever addressed himself to finding number in anything.

Prot. Philebus, I think that what Socrates is now saying is excellent good sense.

18   *Phil.* What he's saying now, yes, so do I. But why, may I ask, is it addressed to us, and what is its purpose?

Soc. A very proper question that, Protarchus, which Philebus has asked us.

Prot. Indeed it is, so do you give him an answer.

Soc. I will do so; but first a small additional point to what I have been saying. When you have got your 'one', you remember, whatever it may be, you must not immediately turn your eyes to the unlimited, but to a number; now the same applies when it is the unlimited that B you are compelled to start with: you must not immediately turn your eyes to the one, but must discern this or that number embracing the multitude, whatever it may be: reaching the one must be the last step of all. We might take our letters again to illustrate what I mean now.

Prot. How so?

Soc. The unlimited variety of sound was once discerned by some god, or perhaps some godlike man; you know the story that there was some such person in Egypt called Theuth. He it was who originally discerned the existence, in that unlimited variety, of the vowels—not 'vowel' in the singular but 'vowels' in the plural—and then of other C things which, though they could not be called articulate sounds, yet were noises of a kind; there were a number of them too, not just one; and as a third class he discriminated what we now call the mutes. Having done that, he divided up the noiseless ones or mutes until he got each one by itself, and did the same thing with the vowels and the intermediate sounds; in the end he found a number of the things, and affixed to the whole collection, as to each single member of it, the name 'letter'. It was because he realised that none of us could ever get to know one of the collection all by itself, in isolation from all the D rest, that he conceived of 'letter' as a kind of bond of unity, uniting as it were all these sounds into one; and so he gave utterance to the expression 'art of letters', implying that there was one art that dealt with the sounds.

18 D–20 C   *Interlude, in which the projected classification of Pleasure
and Knowledge is further postponed*

Socrates now points out the bearing of the foregoing logical digression
on the practical issue. It had been admitted that there are many kinds
of pleasure and of knowledge: we see now that if we are to get to the
bottom of our problem we must discover precisely how many kinds,
and what they are. Protarchus at this becomes exasperated, and
protests against Socrates's impossible demands: instead of discomfiting
others let him undertake the task himself, unless he can see some easier
means of settling the original question.

It is not uncommon for Socrates's interlocutors to make this sort of
protest: cf. *Meno* 80 A, *Hippias Minor* 369 B. Such interludes provide
a respite from hard argument: and this one seems to have the special
purpose of providing Socrates with an excuse for an ostensible shirking
of the projected classification, which, as the reader is warned, is likely
to be a long and difficult business. It is, however, only ostensibly
shirked: we shall come back to it at 31 B. Meantime we shall take up
a point already mooted at 11 D–E, namely the question whether there
may not be a third thing better than either of the claimants originally
presenting themselves as the Human Good.

Philebus   Socrates   Protarchus

Phil. Comparing the illustrations with one another, Protarchus, 18 D
I understand the last one even more clearly than the others; but I still
feel the same dissatisfaction about what has been said as I did a while ago.

Soc. You mean, Philebus, what is the relevance of it all?

Phil. Yes, that is what Protarchus and I have been trying to find
out for a long time.

Soc. Yet surely this that you tell me you have been long trying to
find out is already right in front of you.   E

Phil. How so?

Soc. Our discussion started, didn't it, with the question which of
the two should be chosen, intelligence or pleasure?

Phil. Certainly.

Soc. And of course we can say that each of them is one thing.

Phil. Undoubtedly so.

Soc. Then what the foregoing discourse requires of us is just this,
to show how each of them is both one and many, and how (mind you,
we are not[1] to take the unlimited variety straight away) each possesses
a certain number before the unlimited variety is reached.   19

---

[1] I take μή to indicate a concealed prohibition.

Prot. Philebus, it's no easy problem that Socrates has plunged us into with his curiously roundabout methods. Which of us, do you think, should answer the present question? Perhaps it is a trifle ridiculous that I, after giving a full undertaking to replace you in the discussion, should require you to take the business on again because of my inability to answer the question now put; but it would be far more ridiculous, I think, if neither of us could do so. So what shall we do, B do you think? Socrates, I take it, is now raising the question of kinds of pleasure: has it different kinds, or has it not, and if it has, how many are there and what are they like? And exactly the same question arises with regard to intelligence.

Soc. Precisely, son of Callias. If we are incapable of doing this in respect of everything that is one, like, identical, and is also (as our foregoing account revealed) the opposite, then none of us will ever be any good at anything.

C *Prot.* That's about how it stands, Socrates. Still, though the ideal for a sensible person is to know everything, I fancy it's not such a bad alternative to realise one's own position.[1] Now why do I say that at this moment? I'll tell you. You made all of us a free offer of this discussion, in which you yourself, Socrates, were to share, for the purpose of deciding what is the best of all things possessed by man. When Philebus said pleasure, delight, enjoyment and so forth, you D rejoined that it was not those, but a different kind of things, which we have been glad frequently to remind ourselves of, as we were right to do, so as to have the two kinds of things side by side in our memory while we subject them to examination. What you, I gather, maintain is that there is something which may properly be called a better good than pleasure at all events, namely reason, knowledge, understanding, skill and all that is akin to these things: and that it is these, not pleasure and so on, that we ought to acquire. Now when these two views had been put forward, one maintained against the other, we threatened you E by way of a joke that we would not let you go home until the discussion had been worked out and brought to a satisfactory termination; upon which you agreed to the demand, and allowed us to keep you for that purpose. What we tell you now is, as children say, that you can't take

---

[1] Protarchus means that his position is that of a mere enquirer, who does not promise to solve problems: whereas Socrates has agreed to lead the discussion and promised, at least implicitly, to bring it to a satisfactory conclusion; yet he now apparently expects the others to do the difficult part of the job for him.

back a present once you have duly given it. So stop your present method of dealing with the questions before us.

Soc. What method do you mean?

Prot. That of plunging us into difficulties, and putting questions that 20 it is impossible for us to answer satisfactorily here and now. We ought not to imagine that the object of our present endeavours is to get ourselves all into difficulties; no, if we are incapable of doing the job, it's for you to do it, since you gave your promise. And that being so, please make up your mind for yourself whether you must classify the kinds of pleasure and of knowledge or may pass them over; supposing, that is, that you are able and willing to follow another method and clear up our points of dispute in some other way.

Soc. Well, as you put it like that, there's no need for your poor B victim to expect any further terrors; that 'if you are willing' banishes all my fears on every score. And what's more, I fancy some god has recalled to my mind something that will help us.

Prot. Really? What is it?

Soc. I remember a theory that I heard long ago—I may have dreamt it[1]—about pleasure and intelligence, to the effect that neither of them is the good, but that it is something else, different from either and better than both. Now, you know, if we could get a clear sight of this third thing now, then a victory for pleasure is out of the C question; it couldn't continue to be identical with the good, could it?

Prot. No.

Soc. No, and as to methods for classifying the kinds of pleasure, we shan't need them any longer, I imagine. However, we shall see better as we go on.

Prot. That's good: and may your conclusion be so too.

20 C–22 C   *The good life cannot consist exclusively either of Pleasure or of Intelligence*

Socrates now propounds three qualifications which the Human Good must possess: it must be perfect or complete (τέλεον), adequate (ἱκανόν)

---

[1] We should not look for an earlier author of this theory. It is Plato's own, and the pretence that Socrates remembers it being communicated to him, possibly in a dream, is merely a literary device to call attention to its importance in a way compatible with the character of Socrates, the 'midwife' who can produce no doctrines of his own. The dream-fiction is somewhat similarly employed at *Theaet.* 201 E, where however it introduces not a theory of Plato's own, but possibly of Antisthenes (see Cornford, *Plato's Theory of Knowledge*, p. 144).

and sought after by all who know of it (20 D): this third characteristic is later expressed by the word 'choiceworthy' (αἱρετός, 22 B).

Protarchus readily agrees that a life of nothing but pleasure, if this be understood strictly as excluding all memory of past pleasures, all expectation of those to come, and even the awareness of present pleasure, can possess none of these qualifications. Nor can a life of nothing but intelligence, or cognitive activity in general—a life wholly devoid of both pleasure and pain. All men would certainly prefer a life containing both factors.

The discussion is centred on the notion of choiceworthiness, τὸ αἱρετόν, but it becomes clear that the two lives now rejected lack the other two characteristics as well. Neither can be 'adequate' if each requires supplementing by the other: nor 'perfect' (τέλεος), if it leaves its possessor unsatisfied, not having attained his perfection or end (τέλος).

Plato does not precisely define the words ἱκανός and τέλεος here:[1] but their meanings become clear enough if we compare the discussion in Aristotle, E.N. I 7, 1097 A–B, which is based on the present passage. It is there laid down that Happiness must be τέλειον, i.e. capable of being made an end (τέλος), and that 'the absolutely perfect' (τὸ ἁπλῶς τέλειον) is τὸ καθ᾽ αὑτὸ αἱρετὸν ἀεὶ καὶ μηδέποτε δι᾽ ἄλλο. It is further pointed out that 'self-sufficiency' (τὸ αὔταρκες) is universally admitted to accompany τὸ τέλειον. Aristotle has perhaps given a little more preciseness to the term ἱκανόν by replacing it by αὔταρκες, and he has helpfully interpreted τέλεον (τέλειον) as a particular kind of αἱρετόν.

The upshot then is that of the two rejected lives neither is 'adequate', and so far from being 'perfect' neither is even desirable or choiceworthy.

The modern reader may perhaps feel some unreality in Plato's pressing the isolation of pleasure to the point of actual unawareness that the pleasure is being experienced (τοῦτο αὐτό, εἰ χαίρεις ἢ μὴ χαίρεις, ἀνάγκη δήπου σε ἀγνοεῖν, 21 B). But we shall see later on that he regards one important sort of pleasure as necessarily accompanying, and indeed hardly to be distinguished from, the physiological process of 'replenishment' following upon 'depletion': and this might certainly occur without the consciousness that it is occurring. In any case, whether he be right or wrong, Plato recognises mere feeling, in the sense of pleasure and pain, as other than consciousness of such feeling. Herein he wins the approval of Prof. G. E. Moore, who quotes our present section in the course of an argument against Hedonism: 'Can it really be said that we value pleasure, except in so far as we are conscious of it? Should we think that the attainment of pleasure, of which we never were and never could be conscious, was something to be aimed at for its own sake? It may be impossible that such pleasure should ever exist, that it should ever be thus divorced from

---

[1] Note that 20 D 7–10 is intended to define αἱρετός.

consciousness; although there is certainly much reason to believe that it is not only possible but very common. But, even supposing that it were impossible, that is quite irrelevant. Our question is: Is it the pleasure, as distinct from the consciousness of it, that we set value on?' (*Principia Ethica*, § 52).

I have assumed that the phrase τοῦτο αὐτό...ἀγνοεῖν expresses absolute unawareness of pleasure. It is perhaps possible, however, that Plato does not mean quite as much as this, but rather a condition in which one is aware that one has a feeling but does not know it for pleasure; to know whether one is experiencing a pleasure or not will involve a power of discrimination, which cannot be ascribed to that minimum of cognition which we call 'awareness'. Some support for this alternative interpretation may perhaps be found in the fact that he writes εἰ χαίρεις ἢ μὴ χαίρεις rather than simply ὅτι χαίρεις: and in the recapitulation at 60 D ἡδονήν...ἣν μήτε ἀληθῶς δοξάζοι χαίρειν μήτε τὸ παράπαν γιγνώσκοι τί ποτε πέπονθε πάθος.

Socrates   Protarchus   Philebus

Soc. Well, I should be glad if we could settle a few small points first. 20 C

Prot. What are they?

Soc. Must that which ranks as the good be perfect or imperfect?   D

Prot. The most perfect of all things, Socrates, of course.

Soc. And must the good be adequate also?

Prot. Yes indeed; in fact it must surpass everything in that respect.

Soc. And surely there is one more feature of it that needs stressing, namely that every creature that recognises it goes in pursuit of it, and makes quest of it, desiring to capture it and secure it for its very own, and caring for nothing save such things as involve this or that good[1] in the course of their realisation.

Prot. I cannot but agree with that.

Soc. Now if we're going to have a critical inspection of the life of E pleasure and the life of intelligence, let us see them separately.

Prot. How do you mean?

Soc. Let us have no intelligence in the life of pleasure, and no pleasure in the life of intelligence: for if either of them is the good[2] it

---

[1] ἀγαθοῖς in D 10 is difficult, for we should expect τῷ ἀγαθῷ. But the plural, and the absence of the article, may be due to the fact that Socrates is assuming that there are different chief goods for different species of creatures. This is the more likely inasmuch as the neuter πᾶν τὸ γιγνῶσκον implies that he is generalising, and not at the moment confining his view to the good for man.

[2] If ἀγαθόν is the right reading, it must stand for τἀγαθόν, as at 11 B and 13 E. But the reading of B is ἐστι τἀγαθόν.

must have no need of anything else to be added to it; and if we find
21 that either has such a need, presumably it ceases to be possible for it
to be our true good.

Prot. Quite so.

Soc. Then shall we take you as the subject on which to try our
experiment?

Prot. By all means.

Soc Then here's a question for you.

Prot. Yes?

Soc. Would you care, Protarchus, to live your whole life in the
enjoyment of the greatest pleasures?

Prot. Certainly.

Soc. Then you wouldn't think you needed anything else, if you
had that in the fullest measure?

Prot. I'm sure I shouldn't.

Soc. Now be careful, are you sure you wouldn't need anything in
B the way of thought, intelligence, calculating what is fitting, and so on?

Prot. Why should I? If I had my enjoyment what more could
I want?

Soc. Then if you lived your whole life long like that you would be
enjoying the greatest pleasures, would you?

Prot. Of course.

Soc. But if you were without reason, memory, knowledge, and true
judgment, you would necessarily, I imagine, in the first place be
unaware even whether you were, or were not, enjoying yourself, as
you would be destitute of all intelligence.

Prot. Necessarily.

C   *Soc.* And surely again, if you had no memory you would necessarily,
I imagine, not even remember that you had been enjoying yourself;
of the pleasure you encountered at one moment not a vestige of memory
would be left at the next. Once more, if you had no true judgment
you couldn't judge that you were enjoying yourself when you were;
if you were bereft of the power of calculation you couldn't even
calculate that you would enjoy yourself later on; you would be living
the life not of a human being but of some sort of sea-lung or one of
those creatures of the ocean whose bodies are encased in shells. Am
D I right, or can we imagine the situation to be otherwise?

Prot. We cannot.

Soc. Then is a life like that one that we can desire?

Prot. Your argument, Socrates, has reduced me for the moment to complete speechlessness.

Soc. Well, don't let us lose heart yet; let us turn our attention to the life of reason, and have a look at that.

Prot. What is the 'life of reason'?

Soc. Imagine one of us choosing to live in the possession of intelligence, thought, knowledge and a complete memory of everything, but without an atom of pleasure, or indeed of pain, in a condition of E utter insensibility to such things.

Prot. Neither of these lives seems desirable to me, Socrates, and unless I'm very much mistaken, nobody else will think them so either.

Soc. And what about the combined life, Protarchus, the joint life 22 consisting in a mixture of the two?

Prot. You mean of pleasure, on the one hand, and reason with intelligence on the other?

Soc. Yes, those are the sorts of ingredients I mean.

Prot. Anybody, I imagine, will prefer this mixed life to either of those others. Indeed I will go further: everybody will.

Soc. Then do we realise what result now emerges in our discussion?

Prot. Yes, to be sure: three lives were offered us, and of the first B two neither is sufficient or desirable for any human being or any animal.

Soc. Then surely it is obvious by this time that, if you take these two lives, neither of them proves to contain the good. If it did, it would be sufficient and complete and desirable for all plants and animals that had the capacity of living their lives under such conditions from start to finish; and if any of us preferred something else, he would be mistaking the nature of what is truly desirable, and taking what he never meant to take, as the result of ignorance or some sort of unhappy necessity.

Prot. It certainly looks as if that were so.

Soc. Well then, I think we've said all that needs saying to show that C Philebus's goddess must not be conceived of as identical with the good.

Phil. No, and your 'reason' isn't the good either, Socrates: the case against it looks like being just the same.

Soc. That may well apply to *my* reason, Philebus; not, however, to the true, divine, reason which, I fancy, is in rather a different position.

22 C–23 B   *Which component of the Mixed Life is the cause of its being*
             good? Transition to a metaphysical argument

In his last speech Socrates has caught up Philebus's reference to 'your
reason', and pretends to find in it an implied antithesis between the
reason *belonging to* himself and that belonging to a god. The 'true,
divine reason' may, he suggests, be 'in rather a different position':
this may mean not only what we shall be told at 33 B, that the life of
the gods is devoid of pleasure and pain and their activity that of reason
alone, but perhaps also that νοῦς is the good not of man but of the
universe, in the sense of being the *cause* of its order, beauty, and
goodness, as we shall find it to be in the next section.

It should be noticed that Socrates corrects or modifies his first
suggestion, that reason, rather than pleasure, *is* the cause of the
goodness of the Mixed Life: what he will 'contend with Philebus even
more warmly than before' is that reason is 'nearer and more akin'
than pleasure to 'that, whatever it is, whose possession makes that life
both desirable and good'. The purpose of this modification will become
clear towards the end of the dialogue (65 A–B): what makes the good
life good is neither of its components but the characters of Measure,
Proportion, and Symmetry inherent in its composition: the pleasures
admitted into the good life will themselves display these characters,
but only because, and in so far as, reason by its control imparts and
maintains them.

Thus (to anticipate what will emerge later) the cause of the goodness
in the Mixed Life is twofold; to adopt Aristotle's terminology, the
Formal Cause is the λόγος τῆς μείξεως, the right quantitative relation
between the various kinds of intellectual activity and pleasurable
experience which are admitted; while the Efficient Cause is Reason;
immediately, the controlling reason of the individual man, but ultimately the Cosmic Reason, on which the individual's reason is declared
to be dependent (30 A–c). But to establish the position of νοῦς as
cause and controller we need 'new tactics' and 'different weapons':
we need, in fact, an ontological argument.

                    Socrates   Protarchus

22 c Still I am not arguing at present for the claim of reason to win the first
      prize, as against the combined life; but certainly we ought to look and
   D see what we are going to do about the second prize. For as to the
      cause that makes this combined life what it is, very likely one of us
      will say it is reason, and the other pleasure: so that while neither of the
      two would, on this showing, be the good, one of them might very
      possibly be that which makes the good what it is. This then is the

point for which I will contend with Philebus even more warmly than before: that whatever it is which, by its inclusion in this mixed life, makes that life both desirable and good, it is something to which reason is nearer and more akin than pleasure. If that be so, pleasure E cannot rightly be said to have any sort of claim either to the first prize or to the second; it misses even the third, if we may put any faith in my reasoning at this moment.

Prot. Well yes, Socrates, it does look to me now as if pleasure had been given a knock-out blow by your last arguments; in the fight for the victor's prize she has fallen. But I think we may say that it 23 was prudent of reason not to put in for the first prize, as it would have meant a similar defeat. But if pleasure were to be disappointed of even second prize, she would undoubtedly find herself somewhat slighted by her own admirers: even they wouldn't think her as fair as they did.

Soc. In that case hadn't we better leave her alone, and not cause her pain by subjecting her to the ordeal of a stringent examination?

Prot. That's nonsense, Socrates.

Soc. You mean it's impossible to talk of 'paining pleasure'?   B

Prot. Not so much that, as that you don't realise that none of us will let you go until you have argued this matter out to the end.

Soc. Phew! A considerable business still in front of us, Protarchus, and not exactly an easy one, I should say, to deal with now. It really looks as though I need fresh tactics: if my objective is to secure the second prize for reason I must have weapons different from those of my previous arguments; though possibly some may be the same. Is it to be, then?

Prot. Yes, of course.

23 C–26 D   *Fourfold classification of all existents*

Socrates now proceeds to give a fourfold classification of 'all that now exists in the universe', πάντα τὰ νῦν ὄντα ἐν τῷ παντί. The point of the word 'now' may be to indicate that it is the actual world of our experience that is to be analysed. Socrates is not going to do what Timaeus does, namely to start with a pre-cosmic chaos and reveal its subsequent ordering (διακόσμησις); he will take to pieces what actually exists, and reveal the constituents of the world around us. Whether we accept (with most scholars, ancient and modern) the view that the cosmogony of the *Timaeus* is merely a device of exposition, or follow Aristotle and Plutarch in taking it literally, in either case the *Philebus* method is different, and non-mythical.

The purview of the *Timaeus* is wide; besides accounting for the body and soul of the universe, it has much to say of the physical and psychical make-up of mankind. The *Philebus* seems to contemplate no less wide an analysis: that is to say, the constituents, Limit and Unlimited, which, as we have already (16 c) been told, are found in 'all things that are ever said to be', are here asserted to apply universally: but the assertion is only substantiated and illustrated in a comparatively narrow field, a field whose area is determined by the purpose for which the present ontological section is introduced. The 'new tactics' and 'different weapons' are, as we have seen, adopted in order to establish the function of Cosmic Reason as the causative and controlling factor in the universe, and so indirectly to vindicate the claim of human reason to superiority over pleasure. It will then be enough if we can show a few of the most important and most easily discernible works of Reason: in other words, if we can discover certain instances of the *right* combination (ὀρθὴ κοινωνία, 25 E) of Limit with Unlimited which are manifestly due to the causality of νοῦς. Such right combination necessarily results in good or beautiful products: equable climate and temperature in external Nature, music (i.e. concordant sound), good physical and psychical qualities in man. There is no mention of living beings or of concrete objects, but their omission is natural enough for the reason we have mentioned; and the same is true of the omission of anything evil or imperfect: their mention would be irrelevant, and indeed inimical, to the purpose of the discussion.

But it remains true, and we are meant to see, that there can be κοινωνίαι of Limit and Unlimited that are not 'right'; some degree of Limit is to be found in all things and all conditions of things, and it is just the universality of the two factors that makes Protarchus find it difficult to understand the third class (τὸ γὰρ πλῆθός σε, ὦ θαυμάσιε, ἐξέπληξε τῆς τοῦ τρίτου γενέσεως, 26 C).

In what sense does Reason cause or control the mixture of the two factors? And what is its relation, and their relation, to the Ideas or Forms, whose existence, though not affirmed in the present section, has been involved in the earlier account of classificatory dialectic, and is most certainly not dropped in this stage of Platonism, but on the contrary is re-asserted in the plainest terms both in the account of dialectic later in this dialogue (58–59), and in the approximately contemporary *Timaeus* (48 E, 52 A)?

For the answers to these questions we must go primarily to the *Timaeus* itself, though its interpretation is at many points doubtful owing to the mythical dress in which Plato has chosen to expound his ontology. A commentator on the *Philebus*, in which the ontological passages, despite their obvious importance, are secondary to the ethical and psychological discussion, may perhaps be allowed a certain measure of dogmatism in regard to the *Timaeus*; he must interpret the one dialogue in the light of the other, but he is not called upon to justify his comments at every turn by showing how the one confirms the other, or (as he would perhaps more often find himself doing), by forcing the details of the two works into a doubtful conformity.[1]

So far as the *Philebus* itself answers these questions, it asserts that the element of intelligibility, order, beauty and goodness in the universe is to be found in mathematical determination; it is in and through 'the measures achieved with the aid of the Limit' (26 D) that Reason, which the wise men of old well named 'King of heaven and earth' (28 C), secures the manifestation in the realm of γένεσις of the eternal, the perfect, the ὄντως ὄν. The mixture of the Determinant with the Undetermined (Limit and Unlimited) results in γένεσις εἰς οὐσίαν (26 D), an expression virtually repeated at 27 B, where the 'third kind' is described as ἐκ τούτων τρίτον μεικτὴν καὶ γεγενημένην οὐσίαν. These expressions do not mean or imply that the contents of the μεικτόν are, or include, the Ideas; the instances given are states or conditions of bodies or souls, or of the physical universe, and though these do not cover the whole ground indicated by πάντα τὰ νῦν ὄντα ἐν τῷ παντί there can, in my opinion, be no doubt that the classification intended is a classification of phenomena or γιγνόμενα alone.

How is this to be harmonised with the 'theory of Ideas' as we know it in other dialogues? A vast controversy has raged on this problem, and all the possible answers have, it would seem, been exhausted without any securing general assent. There are insuperable objections, as Dr Bury points out,[2] to a simple identification of the Ideas with the content of any of the four classes; yet one is reluctant to acquiesce without more ado in Prof. Taylor's conclusion that 'it seems plain that the fourfold classification has been devised with a view to a problem where the forms are not specially relevant, and the true solution is thus that they find *no* place in this classification'.[3]

It is obvious that the Ideas cannot be assigned to τὸ ἄπειρον, and hardly less obvious that they cannot belong to τὸ μεικτόν in view of its description as γένεσις. Zeller's view that they are identical with the αἰτία τῆς μείξεως is not indeed so plainly impossible; yet when we find the Cause described at 27 B as τὸ πάντα ταῦτα δημιουργοῦν we are surely justified in seeing a parallel with the δημιουργός of the *Timaeus*, and hence in discriminating it from the Ideas, even as the Demiurge is there[4] explicitly discriminated from them.

---

[1] In my attitude here I think I may claim some support from Prof. Cornford, who has not undertaken a detailed examination of the *Philebus* ontology in *Plato's Cosmology*. I may add that the main points of interpretation in this most valuable book seem to me unquestionably right.

[2] I cannot accept Dr Bury's own solution (pp. lxxii–lxxiv of his Introduction), since it rests on what I think an incorrect assumption, that the cause of the mixture is an 'after-thought, something not provided for in the original scheme'.

[3] *Plato* (1926), p. 417. The view of Sir W. D. Ross (*Arist. Met.* I, p. 171) is that 'Plato appears to be putting forward a fresh analysis whose relation to the ideal theory he has not thought out'.

[4] 28 A–29 A, especially 29 A εἰ μὲν δὴ καλός ἐστιν ὅδε ὁ κόσμος ὅ τε δημιουργὸς ἀγαθός, δῆλον ὡς πρὸς τὸ ἀίδιον ἔβλεπεν.

There remains the class called τὸ πέρας, or τὸ πέρας ἔχον. I shall for the moment set aside the apparent distinction of these two expressions, and ask whether the *Timaeus* lends support to the belief that it is in this class that the Ideas are to be found.

At 52 A the Idea is described as 'not going forth into anything else', and is distinguished in the regular fashion, as invisible, imperceptible and the object of thought, from the perishable, perceptible thing which bears its name, as well as from the τρίτον γένος, the seat of Becoming, elsewhere called the Receptacle (ὑποδοχή), and identified with Space (or rather Place, χώρα). Earlier (50 c) we have been told of 'the things which enter into and pass out of' the Receptacle, and they are described as 'copies of the eternally existent, modelled from them in a fashion hard to explain and marvellous'. These copies of the Ideas are clearly sensible characters or qualities;[1] taken together with the Receptacle they constitute the whole material which the Demiurge takes over and brings from disorder into order (30 A: cf. 53 A πάντα ταῦτ' εἶχεν ἀλόγως καὶ ἀμέτρως) and 'gives a definite shape by means of forms and numbers' (53 B).

It will not be disputed that all this resembles the mixture of πέρας and ἄπειρον by the αἰτία of the *Philebus*. It is true that the *Philebus* speaks of πέρας where the *Timaeus* speaks of 'forms and numbers', and that the 'material' of the *Timaeus* is not called ἄπειρον, though it is said ἀμέτρως ἔχειν and μέτρα are closely associated with πέρας at *Phil.* 26 D, and therefore implicitly excluded from τὸ ἄπειρον. The parallel between the demiurgic Cause of 27 B and the Demiurge of the *Timaeus* has been already noted. The crucial question is how are the Ideas, which the Demiurge 'looks to', the Ideas of which sensible things are copies, related to the εἴδη καὶ ἀριθμοί of 53 B? They cannot be *identified* with these, since they 'go not forth into anything': we must not be misled by that doctrine of the latest Platonism[2] which identifies the Ideas with Numbers.

---

[1] There is a difficulty here. What we should expect to be called τῶν ὄντων ἀεὶ μιμήματα are not those indistinct, disordered characters which have their seat in the Receptacle in the pre-cosmic stage, but sensible objects of ordinary experience, and in particular the four elements in that determinate ordered state into which the Demiurge brings them. It seems probable, however, that at pp. 50–51 Plato either is not able or does not care to keep up the fiction of a Chaos existing in time, before the ordered Cosmos came into being. His immediate concern here is to drive home the conception of a characterless Receptacle, and in particular to distinguish it from the sensible qualities which, entering into it, constitute γένεσις or τὸ γιγνόμενον. This distinction is one that exists both 'before' and 'after' the διακόσμησις; the qualities pass in and out of the Receptacle just as much 'after' as 'before'; hence it is quite intelligible that Timaeus should, by a kind of prolepsis, call them already 'copies of the eternal existents'. As to the following words, τυπωθέντα ἀπ' αὐτῶν τρόπον τινὰ δύσφραστον καὶ θαυμαστόν, ὃν εἰς αὖθις μέτιμεν, I understand this τύπωσις to be the mathematical determination or configuration of 'space *plus* ἴχνη ἄττα (53 B)' which results in the four elements. The account of the τύπωσις is introduced as an ἀήθης λόγος at 53 c, which accords well with its δύσφραστος καὶ θαυμαστὸς τρόπος.

[2] It is a doctrine not found in the dialogues, and I agree with Sir W. D. Ross

There is, it would seem, only one solution, namely to interpret *these* 'forms and numbers' as the 'intermediate mathematical objects' known to us from Aristotle (*Met.* 987 B 15 and elsewhere). The pyramids, octahedra, icosahedra and cubes which constitute the particles of Fire, Air, Water and Earth, and the triangles out of which these are built up, are mathematical entities intermediate between Ideas and Sensibles. Plato, we must suppose, had not fully worked out this doctrine at the time of writing the *Timaeus*: the mode whereby the Sensible is modelled from the Intelligible is δύσφραστος καὶ θαυμαστός: but by interposing this mathematical order of entities, which are at once ἀίδια and πολλά, he finds a means of at once preserving the transcendence of the Idea which 'goes not forth' and of securing an element of order and intelligibility in the things of sense.

Our examination of the *Timaeus* therefore provides no support for an identification of the Ideas with τὸ πέρας: indeed its evidence is clearly against such identification; and we have already refused to find them in the other three classes. Yet it does not necessarily follow that they 'find no place in this classification' in the sense that Plato has left them altogether out of account. Parallelism with the *Timaeus* suggests that νοῦς, the Cause of the mixture, must have a model to look to if it is to secure the 'right association' (25 E) of the two factors. We are not indeed told so, and the reason doubtless is, as Prof. Taylor says, that 'the forms are not specially relevant' to the present problem; though I would rather put it that the mention of them is not specially relevant. This may sound like hair-splitting: but I believe that Plato means us to see that the Ideas are behind the πέρας ἔχοντα in the same way as they are behind the εἴδη καὶ ἀριθμοί of the *Timaeus*, and that they are, as in the *Timaeus*, the model to which Cosmic Reason, τὸ δημιουργοῦν, looks in its causation of the mixture; to a Greek reader the verb δημιουργεῖν would at once imply a model. This interpretation will be the easier to accept if we date the *Timaeus* before the *Philebus*; but that cannot be proved, and we should of course not be justified in using the mere occurrence of the word δημιουργοῦν as an argument for it.

It remains to consider the conceptions of the two factors, τὸ ἄπειρον and τὸ πέρας. A logical application of these Pythagorean terms we have met with in an earlier section (15 D–17 A); there τὸ ἄπειρον meant the indefinite multiplicity of particulars (τὰ πλήθει ἄπειρα), and τὸ πέρας the definite number of species into which they could be put, and as members of which they became accessible to science. In the present section these terms have no longer a logical, but an ontological significance; they are in fact now used in a sense nearer to their proper sense in Pythagorean doctrine. How much Plato has here modified that sense we cannot be sure; but Socrates's words in introducing his

that Ar. *Met.* 1078 B 9–12 means that it was not an original feature of Plato's theory. I think that, if Plato had reached it when he wrote the *Timaeus* and *Philebus*, it could hardly have failed to be found there. Yet in the ἄπειρον and πέρας of the *Philebus* we seem to see it in the making. Cf. Ross, *Aristotle's Metaphysics*, Introd. p. lxix.

account of τὸ ἄπειρον, 'it is a difficult and disputable matter which I bid you examine', suggest that there is some addition or modification. Now Aristotle, in a chapter (*Met.* A 6) in which he notes the points of resemblance and difference between Platonism and Pythagoreanism, says (987 B 25) that the former treated τὸ ἄπειρον as a Dyad of Great and Small instead of as a unity; and this remark is elucidated at *Physics* 206 B 27: 'the reason why Plato made his Indefinite dual is that it is regarded as going further, proceeding indefinitely both towards increase and towards diminution'. In the *Philebus* the term δυάς is not used, but plainly the ἄπειρον is thus conceived. Hot and Cold, Dry and Moist, Fast and Slow, High-pitched and Low-pitched are indefinites (instances of the class τὸ ἄπειρον), because there is no definite point at which an object is hot, cold, etc.: there is no τέλος (terminus) in heat, for what is called hot has always something hotter beyond it, and something less hot short of it. There is in fact a range or continuum of temperature (as of humidity, velocity and pitch), unlimited in both directions; and this feature is brought out by the use here of pairs of antithetical *comparative* adjectives or adverbs—hotter-colder, drier-moister, etc.

Any actual temperature is a definite temperature, which can be expressed quantitatively, and measured on a thermometer; any actual pitch is a definite pitch, expressible quantitatively and measurable on a length of string. This quantity or measure (τὸ ποσόν) is a fixed entity: unlike τὸ ἄπειρον it does not 'advance' but 'stands still' (24 D); it is a point in the continuum. And Plato thinks of the coming into existence of this point as a determining of the continuum by the principle of Limit (τὸ πέρας). This term signifies all mathematical, quantitative determination, which always takes the form of a simple ratio, such as 1 : 1, 2 : 1, 3 : 2. Why should this be so? We do not think of the temperature of our bodies, or the velocity of a wind, as a ratio. The Platonic theory, however, is here influenced by the old Ionian notion of the Opposites; any actual temperature is a mixture of 'the Hot' and 'the Cold' in a certain proportion, so many 'parts' of the one to so many of the other. In the case of pitch, the Pythagorean discovery, that concordant musical notes are expressible as ratios of the lengths of vibrating strings that produce them, lent itself easily to the notion that τὸ ὀξύ and τὸ βαρύ are *mixed* in the ratios of 2 : 1 (Octave), 3 : 2 (Fifth), 4 : 3 (Fourth). Hence Socrates speaks at 25 D–E of the 'Family of the Limit' as 'all that puts an end to the conflict of opposites with one another, making them well-proportioned and harmonious by the introduction of number'.[1]

---

[1] Cf. the account of Pythagorean doctrine quoted from Alexander Polyhistor by Diog. Laert. VIII 26: ἰσόμοιρά τ' εἶναι ἐν τῷ κόσμῳ φῶς καὶ σκότος, καὶ θερμὸν καὶ ψυχρόν, καὶ ξηρὸν καὶ ὑγρόν· ὧν κατ' ἐπικράτειαν θερμοῦ μὲν θέρος γίνεσθαι, ψυχροῦ δὲ χειμῶνα, ξηροῦ δ' ἔαρ, καὶ ὑγροῦ φθινόπωρον· ἐὰν δὲ ἰσομοιρῇ, τὰ κάλλιστα εἶναι τοῦ ἔτους, οὗ τὸ μὲν θάλλον ἔαρ ὑγιεινόν, τὸ δὲ φθίνον φθινόπωρον νοσερόν. This passage contains the germ of Plato's present analysis: a just balance (ἰσομοιρία) of the Opposites constitutes 'the best periods of the year'; cf. 26 B οὐκοῦν..συμμειχθέντων.

Moreover, the mixture of Opposites is at the same time a mixture of πέρας with ἄπειρον. It is this latter sense of μεῖξις that is prominent in our present section; μεικτά are thought of here not primarily as mixtures of Opposites but as products of Limit and Unlimited. But that the former kind of mixture is present to Plato's mind is certain, not only because it is implied by the reference to the warring Opposites at 25 D–E, but from the whole scheme of the dialogue, whose ruling idea is that the Good for man is a mixed life of Pleasure and Intelligence. These are the constituents which have to be mixed in a right proportion: we shall decide, towards the end of the dialogue, how much of the one is to go to how much of the other. Yet within this general scheme of the μεικτὸς βίος Plato will also apply the other kind of mixture, and apply it to Pleasure itself. In this reference Pleasure is an ἄπειρον, which can however be made ἔμμετρον (52 C) in so far as its tendency to indefinite increase (τὸ ἐπὶ τὴν αὔξην ὑπερβάλλειν, as Aristotle puts it) is 'mixed' with a Limit.

It must be admitted that some confusion in the scheme of the dialogue results from these two kinds of μεῖξις. Plato has not discriminated them as clearly as he might, with the result that ἡδονή is sometimes treated as the indeterminate element in feeling, sometimes as actual determinate feeling which can be classified as mental or bodily, pure or impure, true or false.

To denote the second or determinant factor Plato uses τὸ πέρας and τὸ πέρας ἔχον indifferently; at the first mention it is πέρας (23 C), yet at 24 A Socrates refers to 'the entities just mentioned' as τὸ ἄπειρον and τὸ πέρας ἔχον: at 26 B we have τῶν πέρας ἐχόντων, but at 26 C and 27 B τὸ πέρας again. The fact is that πέρας is the class-name for all those ratios that act as determinants: a ratio is a πέρας ἔχον, but Ratio collectively is πέρας; it is perfectly natural to speak of a particular instance of Limit, e.g. 3 : 2 as *having* or *exhibiting* limit: and equally natural to speak of the instances as 'the family of the Limit' (ἡ τοῦ πέρατος γέννα, 25 D) or by a slightly more cumbrous phrase as 'the family of the limit-like' (ἡ τοῦ περατοειδοῦς γέννα, *ibid.*: where the genitive is not, as in the former phrase, one of origin, but one of definition: the γέννα which consists of τὸ περατοειδές).

Socrates   Protarchus

Soc. Let us try to be very careful what starting-point we take.   23 C

Prot. Starting-point?

Soc. Of all that now exists in the universe let us make a twofold division; or rather, if you don't mind, a threefold.

Prot. On what principle, may I ask?

Soc. We might apply part of what we were saying a while ago.

Prot. What part?

Soc. We said, I fancy, that God had revealed two constituents of things, the Unlimited, and the Limit.

Prot. Certainly.

Soc. Then let us take these as two of our classes, and, as the third, D something arising out of the mixture of them both; though I fear I'm a ridiculous sort of person with my sortings of things into classes and my enumerations.

Prot. What are you making out, my good sir?

Soc. It appears to me that I now need a fourth kind as well.

Prot. Tell me what it is.

Soc. Consider the cause of the mixing of these two things with each other, and put down that, please, as number four to be added to the other three.

Prot. Are you sure you won't need a fifth to effect separation?

Soc: Possibly, but not, I think, at the moment. But should the need E arise, I expect you will forgive me if I go chasing after a fifth.[1]

Prot. Yes, to be sure.

Soc. Well then, let us confine our attention in the first place to three out of our four: and let us take two of these three, observing how each of them is split into many and torn apart, and then collecting each of them into one again: and so try to discern in what possible way each of them is in fact both a one and a many.

Prot. Could you make it all a little clearer still? If so, I dare say I could follow you.

24   *Soc.* Well, in putting forward 'two of the three' I mean just what I mentioned a while ago, the Unlimited, and that which has Limit. I will try to explain that in a sense the Unlimited is a many; the Limited may await our later attention.

Prot. It shall.[2]

---

[1] In 23 E 1 perhaps read μεταδιώκοντί ⟨τι⟩ πέμπτον: the loss of τι may have led to the addition of βίου.

The suggestion of a possible 'cause of separation' must be seriously meant, though we hear nothing more of it. Protarchus is no doubt thinking of Empedocles's νεῖκος. It will appear later (25 E ff.) that the only μεικτά that we are concerned with are good states, cosmic or individual; and Plato is probably thinking that he may have occasion to account for the dissolution of these, their loss of πέρας. He would presumably do so not by postulating a malevolent Intelligence, the opposite of νοῦς, but in negative terms, i.e. by the cessation of the operation of νοῦς, as in the myth of the *Statesman* (270 A, 272 E).

It is possible that the suggestion of a fifth factor is due to Plato's predilection for the number 5, noticed by Plutarch, *de E ap. Delph.* 391: compare note on 66 C (p. 140 below).

[2] The English idiom is to use the future here: and possibly we should read μενεῖ.

Soc. Your attention now, please. The matter which I request you to attend to is difficult and controversial, but I request you none the less. Take 'hotter' and 'colder' to begin with, and ask yourself whether you can ever observe any sort of limit attaching to them, or whether these kinds of thing have 'more' and 'less' actually resident in them, so that for the period of that residence there can be no question of B suffering any bounds to be set. Set a term, and it means the term of their own existence.

Prot. That is perfectly true.

Soc. And in point of fact 'more' and 'less' are always, we may assert, found in 'hotter' and 'colder'.

Prot. To be sure.

Soc. Our argument then demonstrates that this pair is always without bounds; and being boundless means, I take it, that they must be absolutely unlimited.

Prot. I feel that strongly, Socrates.

Soc. Ah yes, a good answer, my dear Protarchus, which reminds me that this 'strongly' that you have just mentioned, and 'slightly' C too, have the same property as 'more' and 'less'. When they are present in a thing they never permit it to be of a definite quantity, but introduce into anything we do the character of being 'strongly' so-and-so as compared with 'mildly' so-and-so, or the other way round. They bring about a 'more' or a 'less', and obliterate definite quantity. For, as we were saying just now, if they didn't obliterate definite quantity, but permitted definite and measured quantity to find D a place where 'more and less' and 'strongly and slightly' reside, these latter would find themselves turned out of their own quarters. Once you give definite quantity to 'hotter' and 'colder' they cease to be; 'hotter' never stops where it is but is always going a point further, and the same applies to 'colder'; whereas definite quantity is something that has stopped going on and is fixed. It follows therefore from what I say that 'hotter', and its opposite with it, must be unlimited.

Prot. It certainly looks like it, Socrates; though, as you said, these matters are not easy to follow. Still, if things are said again and yet E again, there is some prospect[1] of the two parties to a discussion being brought to a tolerable agreement.

Soc. Quite right: that's what we must try to do. However, for the

---

[1] It seems necessary to read τά for τό in D 9. ἴσως is to be taken, by hyperbaton, with ἂν ἀποφήναιεν.

present, to avoid going over the whole long business, see whether we can accept what I shall say as a mark of the nature of the Unlimited.

Prot. What is it then?

Soc. When we find things becoming 'more' or 'less' so-and-so, or admitting of terms like 'strongly', 'slightly', 'very' and so forth, we 25 ought to reckon them all as belonging to a single kind, namely that of the Unlimited; that will conform to our previous statement, which was, if you remember, that we ought to do our best to collect all such kinds as are torn and split apart, and stamp a single character on them.

Prot. I remember.

Soc. Then things that don't admit of these terms, but admit of all the opposite terms like 'equal' and 'equality' in the first place, and then 'double' and any term expressing a ratio of one number to another, B or one unit of measurement to another, all these things we may set apart and reckon—I think we may properly do so—as coming under the Limit. What do you say to that?

Prot. Excellent, Socrates.

Soc. All right. Now what description are we going to give of number three, the mixture of these two?

Prot. That, I think, will be for you to tell me.

Soc. Or rather for a god to tell us, if one comes to listen to my prayers.

Prot. Then offer your prayer, and look to see if he does.

Soc. I am looking; and I fancy, Protarchus, that one of them has befriended us for some little time.[1]

C *Prot.* Really? What makes you believe that?

Soc. I'll explain, of course: please follow what I say.

Prot. Pray go on.

Soc. We spoke just now, I believe, of 'hotter' and 'colder', did we not?

Prot. Yes.

Soc. Now add to these 'drier and wetter', 'higher and lower',[2]

---

[1] The suggestion of divine inspiration here seems to mean that Plato is conscious of grafting something novel on to Pythagoreanism. The novelty consists in regarding the mixture as effected by νοῦς, and therefore as resulting in *good* states only. Thus Plato playfully justifies by a divine 'guidance' his deliberate restriction of μεικτά, a restriction dictated by the *purpose* of the ontological analysis.

[2] The words in fact mean 'more and less in quantity': but 'more and less' must be kept in an English translation for μᾶλλόν τε καὶ ἧττον in C 10.

'quicker and slower', 'greater and smaller', and everything that we brought together a while ago as belonging to that kind of being which admits of 'the more' and 'the less'.

Prot. You mean the kind that is unlimited?   D

Soc. Yes. And now, as the next step, combine with it the family of the Limit.

Prot. What is that?

Soc. The one we omitted to collect just now; just as we collected the family of the Unlimited together, so we ought to have collected that family which shows the character of Limit; but we didn't.[1] Still perhaps it will come to the same thing in spite of that, if in the process of collecting these two kinds the family we have spoken of is going to become plain to view.

Prot. What family? Please explain.

Soc. That of 'equal' and 'double', and any other that puts an end to the conflict of opposites with one another, making them well- E proportioned and harmonious by the introduction of number.

Prot. I see: by mixing in these[2] you mean, apparently, that we find various products arising as they are respectively mixed.

Soc. You take my meaning aright.

Prot. Then continue.

---

[1] The assertion that there has been no συναγωγή of ἡ τοῦ πέρατος (or τοῦ περατοειδοῦς) γέννα means (as Badham quoted by Bury, p. 168, says) that 'we have had nothing to answer to ὑγρότερον καὶ ξηρότερον and the other examples'. That is to say, Socrates has not told us *what* ratio introduced into the Hotter-and-Colder will constitute a normal temperature of our bodies, or *what* ratio of Wetter-and-Drier will make an equable climate, or *what* ratio of Higher-and-Lower will produce the concord of the Fifth. But I cannot follow Bury in his explanation of the reason for the absence of this συναγωγή. It is omitted, I think, merely as being unnecessary and unimportant: it would have been very tedious to give a list of all the particular ratios involved in all the cases of μεικτά mentioned. On the other hand, it is perfectly true that, as Socrates says, when we know the particular ἄπειρον and the particular μεικτόν the particular πέρας ἔχον will be clear enough. By this is meant, not that when we perceive that Health and Concord involve numerical ratios we at once know what those ratios must be, but that these cases of μεικτά enable us readily to grasp the abstract principle of πέρας in and through its manifestation in these several spheres.

As to the text of 25 D7-8 the insertion of εἰ with Vahlen and Burnet seems all that is needed. τούτων ἀμφοτέρων means 'these other two' (as distinguished from ἡ τοῦ περατοειδοῦς γέννα)—namely τὸ ἄπειρον and τὸ μεικτόν: and ἐκείνη means ἡ τοῦ πέρατος (or τοῦ περατοειδοῦς) γέννα. Protarchus's repeated ποίαν refers to this last. There is no difference between ἡ τοῦ πέρατος γέννα and ἡ τοῦ περατοειδοῦς γέννα, except that in the former the genitive is one of origin, in the latter one of definition.

[2] μειγνύς = immiscens (*not* in unum commiscens) and ταῦτα means the πέρατος γέννα, of which instances have just been given. αὐτῶν in the next line has the same reference as ταῦτα.

48 PHILEBUS

Soc. In cases of sickness does not the right association of these factors¹ bring about health?

26 *Prot.* Unquestionably.

Soc. And in the case of high and low in pitch, or of swift and slow, which are unlimited, does not the introduction² of these same elements at once produce limit and establish the whole art of music in full perfection?

Prot. Admirably put.

Soc. And then again, if they are introduced where there is severe cold and stifling heat they remove all that is excessive and unlimited, and create measure and balance.

Prot. Certainly.

B *Soc.* Then it is here that we find the source of fair weather and all other beautiful things, namely in a mixture of the unlimited with that which has limit?

Prot. Of course.

Soc. And indeed there are countless more things which I may omit to enumerate, such as beauty and strength along with health, besides a whole host of fair things found in our souls. For that goddess of ours,³ fair Philebus, must have observed the lawlessness and utter wickedness of mankind due to an absence of limit in men's pleasures and appetites, and therefore established amongst them⁴ a law and order that are marked by limit. You maintain that she thereby spoiled them:

c I assert that on the contrary she preserved them. What do you think about it, Protarchus?

Prot. I am thoroughly satisfied, Socrates.

Soc. Well, there are the three things I have spoken of, if you follow me.

Prot. Yes, I think I see what you mean. You are asserting, I gather, two factors in things: first the Unlimited, second the Limit. But

¹ τούτων probably means the two 'kinds' (πέρας and ἄπειρον); though in order to secure for it the same reference as for ταῦτα in E 3 and ταὐτὰ ταῦτα in 26 A 3 we might possibly take ἡ τούτων ὀρθὴ κοινωνία to mean 'the right sharing (sc. by the ἄπειρα) in these' (sc. πέρας ἔχοντα).

² I retain ἐγγιγνόμενα and remove the colon after ταῦτα. ταὐτὰ ταῦτα means the ratios (πέρας ἔχοντα, πέρατος γέννα). It is illogical to say that their introduction produces πέρας, but apparently the word is used carelessly for ἐμμετρίαν or συμμετρίαν: cf. τὸ ἔμμετρον καὶ ἅμα σύμμετρον ἀπηργάσατο in A 7.

³ The identity of this goddess, who has the function, shortly to be assigned to νοῦς, of effecting the mixture, or imposing limit, is probably meant to be left vague. She may be Harmonia, but her sex is due simply to the wish to provide a counterblast to Philebus's Aphrodite-Hedone at 12 B.

⁴ Reading ἐνέθετο, suggested by Bury.

I can't altogether grasp what you mean by the third thing that you mention.

Soc. The reason for that, my dear good sir, is that you are confused by the multiplicity of that third kind. And yet a plurality of forms were presented by the Unlimited too, and in spite of that we stamped on them the distinguishing mark of 'the more' and its opposite, and D so saw them as a unity.

Prot. True.

Soc. Then again we did not complain about the Limit, either that it exhibited[1] a plurality, or that it was not a real unity.

Prot. No, there was no reason to do so.

Soc. None whatever. And now as to the third kind, I am reckoning all this progeny of our two factors as a unity, and you may take me to mean a coming into being,[2] resulting from those measures that are achieved with the aid of the Limit.

Prot. I understand.

26 E–31 B   *The affinity of Intelligence to the Cosmic Cause, and to the cause of goodness in the Mixed Life*

We now pass to the fourth 'kind', the efficient cause of the Mixture, that is to say the Universal or Cosmic cause of all that comes into being. If it can be proved that this cause does in fact exist, and that it is an Intelligence working for good ends, we shall have ground for asserting that man's intelligence, as a constituent of the Mixed Life of the individual, is more akin to the cause of that life's goodness than is pleasure. This is what we had set out to prove at 22 D.

The result of the present section is not that *our* intelligence makes the Mixed Life good: it is the Cosmic Reason that does so, operating as an external efficient cause which imposes Limit on the Unlimited and thereby gives that life its συμμετρία; yet there is the closest relation

---

[1] I accept Bury's ⟨ὅτι⟩ before πολλά.

[2] I agree with Prof. G. M. A. Grube (*Plato's Thought*, p. 303) that we should not read too much into the words γένεσιν εἰς οὐσίαν. οὐσία is not infrequently used of the being or existence of ordinary things (γιγνόμενα). Thus *Soph.* 219 B speaks of πᾶν ὅπερ ἂν μὴ πρότερόν τις ὂν ὕστερον εἰς οὐσίαν ἄγῃ, *Theaet.* 186 B of the οὐσία of τὸ σκληρόν and τὸ μαλακόν (hard and soft objects), and *Tim.* 35 A of τῆς ἀμερίστου καὶ ἀεὶ κατὰ ταὐτὰ ἐχούσης οὐσίας καὶ τῆς αὖ περὶ τὰ σώματα γιγνομένης μεριστῆς. It follows that γένεσις εἰς οὐσίαν need not mean anything more than γένεσις alone. Similarly with the phrase ἐκ τούτων τρίτον μεικτὴν καὶ γεγενημένην οὐσίαν (27 B); I do not think Plato means us to find any ontological significance in the collocation of the last two words; it is merely 'the kind of existence which is the mixture or product of these two' (sc. πέρας and ἄπειρον). It may be added that the phrase is often misleadingly quoted without the words ἐκ τούτων, which of course belong to γεγενημένην as much as to μεικτήν.

between this νοῦς and our own. If not explicitly stated, it is certainly implied that our νοῦς is derived from and dependent on the Cosmic Reason, just as our bodies are derived from the Body of the universe, and our souls from its Soul. Precisely how such derivation or dependence is to be conceived Plato does not tell us: he seems indeed carefully to refrain from saying that the human reason is *part* of the divine, and the dominating notion with which he works here is that of affinity or similarity.

If the metaphysical doctrine thus lacks completeness, we should again remember that it is introduced not for its own sake, but for an ethical purpose. Nevertheless the doctrine of a Cosmic Intelligence 'resident' in a Cosmic Soul is here argued with such zest as to show that Plato sets great store by it; it is in fact a doctrine which assumes increasing importance in his mind from the moment when, in the *Sophist* (248 E), he proclaims through the mouth of the Eleatic Stranger that Life, Soul and Wisdom belong to 'that which is perfectly real': it is a doctrine elaborated in the *Timaeus* and *Laws* x.

The nerve of the argument here is the parallel of microcosm and macrocosm. Our bodily elements are visibly and patently fragments of the physical elements in the universe; correspondingly we must derive our souls from a World-soul. And if our souls contain Reason, can we deny that to the World-soul?

There is nothing essentially new in this argument, and indeed Plato clearly acknowledges his debt to earlier thinkers. 'All the wise agree that Reason is king of heaven and earth.' That Anaxagoras is one laid under contribution is obvious; another may well be Diogenes of Apollonia.[1] In the *Memorabilia* (1 4) Xenophon attributes to Socrates proofs of divine Providence which depend partly on the microcosm-macrocosm argument, and in places the language is very similar to that found here.[2]

Socrates   Protarchus   Philebus

26E   *Soc.* And now to continue: we said that besides the three kinds there is a fourth kind to be considered: and it is for our joint consideration. Now I expect you regard it as necessary that all things that come to be should come to be because of some cause.

Prot. Yes, I do; without that how could they come to be?

Soc. Well, is there anything more than a verbal difference between a cause and a maker? Wouldn't it be proper to call that which makes things and that which causes them one and the same?

Prot. Quite proper.

---

[1] See his Fragg. 4 and 5 (Diels) and compare Diès, *Autour de Platon*, p. 533.
[2] Cf. e.g. *Mem.* 1, 4, §§ 8, 13 and 17 with *Phil.* 29 C and 30 B.

Soc. And further, shall we find that between that which is made 27
and that which comes to be there is, once again, a mere verbal
difference?

Prot. Yes.

Soc. And isn't it natural that that which makes should have the
leading position, while that which is made follows in its train when
coming into being?

Prot. Certainly.

Soc. Hence a cause and that which, as a condition of coming to be,
is subservient to a cause, are not the same but different?

Prot. Of course.

Soc. Now our three kinds gave us all things that come to be, and
the constituents from which they come to be, did they not?

Prot. Quite so.

Soc. And this fourth kind that we are speaking of, which fashions B
all these things, this cause, is pretty clearly different from them?

Prot. Yes, different certainly.

Soc. But now that the four kinds have been discriminated it will do
no harm to enumerate them in order, so that we may remember each
by itself.

Prot. I agree.

Soc. The first, then, I call the Unlimited, the second the Limit, and
the third the being that has come to be by the mixture of these two;
as to the fourth, I hope I shall not be at fault in calling it the cause of C
the mixture and of the coming to be?

Prot. No indeed.

Soc. Come along now: what is our next point, and what was our
purpose in getting where we have got? Wasn't it that we were trying
to find out whether the second prize would go to pleasure or to
intelligence? Was not that it?

Prot. Yes, it was.

Soc. Then shall we perhaps be in a better position, now that we have
discriminated these kinds as we have, to achieve our decision about the
first place and the second? For that of course was what we started to
dispute about.

Prot. Perhaps.

Soc. Come on then. We laid it down, I think, that victory went to D
the mixed life of pleasure and intelligence. Was that so?

Prot. It was.

Soc. Then of course we can see what kind of life this is and to which kind it belongs?

Prot. Undoubtedly.

Soc. In fact we shall assert, I suppose, that it is a part of our third kind.[1] For that kind does not consist of just two things, but of all unlimited things bound fast by the Limit; hence it is correct to make our victorious life a part of it.

Prot. Yes, perfectly correct.

E   *Soc.* Very well. And what about your pleasant unmixed life, Philebus? Under which of the kinds that we have mentioned should we be correct in saying that that falls? But before you express your view let us have your answer to a question I will put.

Phil. Please put it.

Soc. Do pleasure and pain contain a Limit, or are they amongst the things that admit of 'the more' and 'the less'?

Phil. They are, Socrates: they admit of 'the more'. Pleasure would not be supremely good,[2] if it were not of its very nature unlimited both in quantity and degree.

28   *Soc.* And similarly, Philebus, pain would not be supremely bad; hence we must look for something other than the character of being unlimited to explain how an element of good attaches to pleasures. Well, we may leave that topic, if you please, as one of unlimited speculation.[3] But I will ask both of you, in which of our above-mentioned kinds may we now reckon intelligence, knowledge and reason, without sinning against the light? I fancy a great deal turns

[1] It may be objected that nothing has been said to show, or even to suggest, that the Mixed Life is a mixture of Limit and Unlimited: and that though the assertion may be half substantiated by the immediately following declaration (which gets at least some show of proof) that Pleasure belongs to the ἄπειρον class, yet the other constituent, Intelligence, is not declared to belong to πέρας, but to be akin to the fourth 'kind', viz. the αἰτία.

It must, I think, be admitted that there is some confusion here, resulting from the twofold application of the term μεῖξις already noted. Yet there can be no doubt that Plato conceives of human intelligence as setting a limit to the 'unlimited advance' of Pleasure, keeping it within bounds; the curiously unexpected use of δεδεμένων at 27 D 9 suggests this, and it is of course in accordance with the regular Socratico-Platonic notion of the control of Desire (ἐπιθυμία, which, as Aristotle says, is ὄρεξις τοῦ ἡδέος) by Reason. But this line of thought is not pursued here; for it is the superiority of Intelligence to Pleasure that Plato is concerned to prove: and to prove that he must assign it to the fourth 'kind', not the second.

[2] I accept Bekker's πανάγαθον in E 8 and πάγκακον in A 1.

[3] Paley and Apelt are doubtless right in seeing a play on words; ἀπεράντων (unfinished, unsettled in discussion) suggests ἀπείρων (unlimited). This can hardly be reproduced in translation. I read with Bury τοῦτο... γεγονὸς ἔστω.

on our present enquiry, according as we give the right answer or the wrong.

Phil. You are glorifying your own god, Socrates.　　　　　　B

Soc. And you your own goddess, my friend; still we ought to give an answer to our question.

Prot. Socrates is right, you know, Philebus; we must do as he tells us.

Phil. Well, you have volunteered to speak on my behalf, have you not, Protarchus?

Prot. Certainly; but at the moment I am rather at a loss, and beg you, Socrates, to state the case to us yourself; otherwise you may find us striking a false note and making mistakes about your candidate.

Soc. I must do as you say, Protarchus; as a matter of fact it is no c difficult task you impose on me. But did I really cause you alarm by my playful glorification, as Philebus has called it, when I asked you to which kind reason and knowledge belong?

Prot. Very much so, Socrates.

Soc. But really it's an easy question. For all the wise agree (thereby glorifying themselves in earnest) that in Reason we have the king of heaven and earth. And I fancy they are right. But I should like us, if you don't mind, to make a fuller investigation of the kind in question itself.

Prot. Proceed as you like, Socrates, and please feel no concern about D being lengthy; we shan't quarrel with you.

Soc. Thank you. Then let us begin, shall we, by putting the following question.

Prot. What is it?

Soc. Are we to say, Protarchus, that the sum of things or what we call this universe is controlled by a power that is irrational and blind, and by mere chance, or on the contrary to follow our predecessors in saying that it is governed by Reason and a wondrous regulating Intelligence?

Prot. A very different matter,[1] my dear good Socrates. What you E are suggesting now seems to me sheer blasphemy. To maintain that Reason orders it all does justice to the spectacle of the ordered universe, of the sun, the moon, the stars and the revolution of the whole heaven;

---

[1] οὐδὲν τῶν αὐτῶν indicates the difference between this and the previous question. Protarchus had hesitated about the 'kind' to which Reason should be assigned: he has no hesitation between the two alternatives now proposed.

and for myself I should never express nor conceive any contrary view on the matter.

Soc. Then are you willing that we should assent to what earlier
29 thinkers agree upon, that this is the truth? And ought we not merely to think fit to record the opinions of other people without any risk to ourselves, but to participate in the risk and take our share of censure when some clever person asserts that the world is not as we describe it, but devoid of order?

Prot. I am certainly willing to do so.

Soc. Come then, and direct your attention to the point that confronts us next.

Prot. What is it, please?

Soc. We can discern certain constituents of the corporeal nature of all animals, namely fire, water, breath, and 'earth too like storm-tossed sailors we discern', as the saying goes: these are all present in their composition.

B   *Prot.* Quite so: and storm-tossed in truth we are by difficulty in our present discussion.

Soc. Well now, let me point out to you something that applies to each of these elements in our make-up.

Prot. What?

Soc. In each case it is only an inconsiderable fragment that is in us, and that too very far from being pure in quality or possessing a power befitting its real nature. Let me explain to you in one instance, which you must regard as applying to them all. There is fire, is there not, belonging to ourselves, and again fire in the universe?

Prot. Of course.

C   *Soc.* And isn't the fire that belongs to ourselves small in quantity and weak and inconsiderable, whereas the fire in the universe is wonderful in respect of its mass, its beauty, and all the powers that belong to fire?

Prot. What you say is perfectly true.

Soc. And to continue, is the universal fire sustained and produced and increased by the fire that belongs to us, or is the opposite true, that my fire and yours and that of all other creatures owe all this to that other?

Prot. That question doesn't even merit an answer.

D   *Soc.* You are right; indeed I imagine you will say the same about the earth that we have here in creatures and the earth in the universe, and in fact about all the elements that I mentioned in my question a moment ago. Will your answer be as I suppose?

Prot. Could anyone giving a different answer be deemed right in his head?

Soc. I hardly think so, whoever he were. But come with me now to the next point. If we regard all these elements that I have been speaking of as a collective unity we give them, do we not, the name of body?

Prot. Of course.

Soc. Well, let me point out that the same holds good of what we E call the ordered universe; on the same showing it will be a body, will it not, since it is composed of the same elements?

Prot. You are quite right.

Soc. Then, to put it generally, is the body that belongs to us sustained by this body of the universe, has it derived and obtained therefrom all that I referred to just now, or is the converse true?

Prot. That is another question, Socrates, that doesn't deserve to be put.

Soc. Well, does this one then? I wonder what you will say. 30

Prot. Tell me what it is.

Soc. Shall we not admit that the body belonging to us has a soul?

Prot. Plainly we shall.

Soc. And where, Protarchus my friend, could it have got it from, if the body of the universe, which has elements the same as our own though still fairer in every respect, were not in fact possessed of a soul?

Prot. Plainly there can be no other source, Socrates.

Soc. No, for surely we cannot suppose, Protarchus, that those four kinds, Limit, Unlimited, Combined and Cause, which is present in all things as a fourth kind—we cannot suppose that this last-named, while B on the one hand it furnishes the elements that belong to our bodies with soul, maintains our physique and cures a body when it has come to harm, and provides all sorts of arrangements and remedial measures, in virtue of all which we recognise it as Wisdom in all her diverse applications, has nevertheless failed in the case of the elements of the universe (although they are these same elements that pervade the whole heaven on a great scale, fair moreover and untainted), failed, I say, there to contrive that which is fairest and most precious.[1]

---

[1] The text in this long sentence needs no emendation. The absence of articles with πέρας, ἄπειρον and κοινόν is no more difficult than at 30 c: and the fact that

c *Prot.* No. to suppose that would be utterly unreasonable.

Soc. Discarding that, then, we should do better to follow the other view and say, as we have said many times already, that there exist in the Universe much 'Unlimited' and abundance of 'Limit', and a presiding Cause of no mean power, which orders and regulates the years, the seasons and the months, and has every claim to the names of Wisdom and Reason.

Prot. Every claim indeed.

Soc. But Wisdom and Reason cannot come into existence without soul.

Prot. They cannot.

d *Soc.* Hence you will say that in the nature of Zeus a royal soul and a royal reason come to dwell by virtue of the power of the Cause, while in other gods other perfections dwell, according to the names by which they are pleased to be called.[1]

Protarchus asks at 31 c to be *reminded* of what κοινόν means is not an argument for excising reference to it here but for preserving it. The anacoluthon involved in starting with the four kinds as subjects to the succeeding infinitives, and then restricting the subject to the fourth kind alone, is not unnatural, and has the effect and purpose of emphasising that the four kinds cover not only τὰ παρ' ἡμῖν but the whole physical universe. τῶν αὐτῶν τούτων refers not (as Bury thinks) to the four kinds but to the τὰ παρ' ἡμῖν of B 1, i.e. to the four 'elements' (cf. 29 B 6–8).

The last words 'that which is fairest and most precious' refer to a Cosmic soul or souls. τὴν τῶν καλλίστων καὶ τιμιωτάτων φύσιν is a common periphrasis for τὰ κάλλιστα καὶ τιμιώτατα: but why the plural? Because Plato wavers between a single world-soul animating the whole universe and a plurality animating its several parts (sun, moon, heaven of fixed stars, planets); cf. *Laws* 898 c ff., especially c 7 ἢ πᾶσαν ἀρετὴν ἔχουσαν ψυχὴν μίαν ἢ πλείους. Apart from the present sentence he adheres, in our dialogue, to the hypothesis of a single world-soul.

The argument is this: Even apart from the need to postulate a world-soul as the source of our own souls (30 A 5–8) it would be unreasonable to believe that the Cause which animates our bodies, and enables them to maintain or regain health, should fail to animate and sustain the body of the universe. And this Cause, both in ourselves and in the universe, is, in virtue of such activity, an intelligent Cause, working for good ends: it is σοφία or νοῦς.

That the αἰτία, by mixing πέρας and ἄπειρον, causes health and 'countless fair things in our souls' we have been told already (25 E–26 B): its designation here as νοῦς is a natural corollary. What is perhaps surprising is the statement that it animates our bodies, puts soul into them (ἐν τοῖς παρ' ἡμῖν ψυχὴν παρέχον). But Plato feels it natural to assume that, once we have reached the conception of an Intelligence as cosmic cause, the actual giving of *life*—the powers of cognition and self-movement—to living creatures must be included in its activity. If the *Timaeus* was already known to his readers, they would remember that the Demiurge there constructs the World-Soul by a mixture of certain ingredients, and that human souls are similarly constructed by the created star-gods from the residue of these ingredients. *This* mixture is not of πέρας and ἄπειρον, but of οὐσία ταὐτόν and θάτερον. But Plato cannot give all his doctrine everywhere.

[1] Taking this at its face-value, we have a sharp distinction drawn between a transcendent αἰτία (which at c 6 was identified with σοφία καὶ νοῦς) and a νοῦς immanent in the universe as a part or character of the world-soul. And it may

Prot. Quite so.

Soc. Now don't suppose, Protarchus, that we have spoken of this matter purposelessly; on the contrary it supports those ancient thinkers that we mentioned, who declared that Reason always rules all things

Prot. Yes indeed it does.

Soc. And, what's more, it has provided an answer to my enquiry, to the effect that mind belongs to the family[1] of what we called the E

seem harsh that in two successive sentences (c 6 and c 9) Socrates should use the collocation σοφία καί νοῦς first with a transcendent, then with an immanent reference.

Although we may admit that Plato has not expressed his meaning with perfect lucidity, yet the difficulty largely disappears if we realise that the distinction is one of aspect rather than of being. Transcendent νοῦς and immanent νοῦς are not two different Reasons: the latter is the self-projection of the former. It is *qua* projected that νοῦς must be οὐκ ἄνευ ψυχῆς, just as at *Tim.* 30 B the Demiurge is said to have found that νοῦν χωρίς ψυχῆς ἀδύνατον παραγενέσθαι τῳ. Proclus (*in Tim.* I, p. 402, Diehl) has understood this: εἰ ἄρα δεῖ τὸ πᾶν ἔννουν γενέσθαι, δεῖ καὶ ψυχῆς· ὑποδοχὴ γάρ ἐστιν αὕτη τοῦ νοῦ, καὶ δι' αὐτῆς ὁ νοῦς ἐμφαίνεται τοῖς ὄγκοις τοῦ παντός, οὐχ ὅτι δεῖται τῆς ψυχῆς ὁ νοῦς· οὕτω γὰρ ἂν ἀτιμότερος εἴη τῆς ψυχῆς· ἀλλ' ὅτι τὰ σώματα δεῖται τῆς ψυχῆς εἰ μέλλει νοῦ μεθέξειν. Similarly Zeller, II i, p. 715, Note 1: 'Es handelt sich hierbei' (viz. *Tim.* 30 B, *Phil.* 30 C) 'nicht um die Vernunft in ihren überweltlichem Sein, sondern um die Vernunft wiefern sie dem Weltganzen (mythisch ausgedrückt: der Natur des Zeus) inwohnt; von dieser innerweltlichen Vernunft aber wird die überweltliche noch unterschieden, wenn es heisst, Zeus besitze eine königliche Seele und einen königliche Verstand διὰ τὴν τῆς αἰτίας δύναμιν.' In the last half of this sentence Zeller appears to find (in my opinion, wrongly) a more absolute distinction in D 1–3 than in c 9–10: but the first half seems to express Plato's meaning correctly.

That he interprets the 'nature of Zeus' rightly may be inferred from the very similar language and structure of *Tim.* 30 B: κατὰ λόγον τὸν εἰκότα δεῖ λέγειν τόνδε τὸν κόσμον ζῷον ἔμψυχον ἔννουν τε τῇ ἀληθείᾳ διὰ τὴν τοῦ θεοῦ γενέσθαι πρόνοιαν. The mention of 'other gods' is no more than a conventional concession to current belief, and we should not press for an identification of them.

[1] Reading γενεᾶς for γένους in 30 E 1. Cf. 66 B πάνθ' ὁπόσα τῆς γενεᾶς αὖ ταύτης ἐστίν, and 52 C–D, τῆς τοῦ ἀπείρου...θῶμεν αὐτὰς εἶναι γένους, where, as here, τῆς requires a feminine noun, and Badham proposed γενεᾶς. Certain Neoplatonist and modern scholars think that Plato coined a word γενούστης with the meaning of γεννήτης or συγγενής, and that this coinage is the 'joke' alluded to by Socrates just below. The joke would, I think, be a poor one, and it is not easy to see how and when Protarchus is supposed to become aware of it.

When Protarchus says 'Though I hadn't realised (sc. until you pointed it out this moment) you had answered the question' he means that he had failed to see that the whole ontological 'digression' (from 23 c onwards) was designed to answer the question whether Intelligence or Pleasure deserved the 'second prize'. Socrates replies that one occasionally relieves the strain of serious argument by a playful interlude. This is ironical: the playful interlude (i.e. the whole onto-logical section) has the great importance of many Platonic 'digressions'; cf. *Phaedrus*, 265 c, where the whole μυθικὸς ὕμνος is called a παιδιά; *Rep.* 536 c, where, in reference to his passionately serious defence of Philosophy, Socrates says ἐπελαθόμην ὅτι ἐπαίζομεν. Moreover at 28 c above he has called his 'glorification' of Reason a piece of playfulness.

It is difficult to be certain what kind of a genitive τοῦ...λεχθέντος is. I think it is probably one of origin: each human mind is a member of the family whose head or parent is the Cosmic Cause.

cause of all things. By this time, I imagine, you grasp what our answer is.

Prot. Yes, I grasp it completely: though indeed I hadn't realised you had given it.

Soc. Well, Protarchus, playfulness is sometimes a relief from seriousness.

Prot. You are right.

31 *Soc.* I think, my friend, that we have now arrived at a fairly satisfactory demonstration of what kind Reason[1] belongs to, and what function it possesses.

Prot. I am sure of it.

Soc. And as for Pleasure's kind, that we found some time ago.

Prot. Exactly.

Soc. Then let us have these points in mind about the pair of them, namely that reason was found akin to Cause and belonging, we may say, to that kind, whereas pleasure is itself unlimited and belongs to the kind that does not and never will contain within itself and derived from itself either beginning, or middle, or end.

B *Prot.* We shall bear that in mind, naturally.

31 B–32 B   *Pleasure as replenishment of wastage*

We now embark on the classification of pleasures, which was seen to be necessary long since, but has been deferred until various preliminary problems have been disposed of. It is not indeed formally announced that the classification now begins; what we are told is that we must discover the *seat* of Pleasure and Pain, and the experience (πάθος) which gives rise to them. But it will become apparent, as we proceed, that the experiences, and correspondingly the pleasures themselves, are of various kinds.

The first kind, discussed in the present section, is that which attends on the process whereby the equilibrium of a physical organism that has been upset is restored, or a depletion replenished. This account of pleasure has its roots, as Prof. Taylor points out,[2] in Alcmaeon's doctrine of health as the due balance (ἰσονομία) of the bodily Opposites, and in the further development which, as we can see from the *Gorgias* (493 A ff.), has been added by the Pythagoreans. The desire for pleasure, as Socrates there points out to Callicles, is a desire for 'filling-up' (πλήρωσις), replenishing a wastage. Such replenishment is therefore attended by pleasure, while the opposite process of wastage is attended

---

[1] Reading νοῦς δήπου with Bekker and Bury, to get the required antithesis with ἡδονῆς in A 5.

[2] *Commentary on Plato's Timaeus*, p. 448.

by pain. Hence eating, as a πλήρωσις, can actually be called ἡδονή (31 E), not of course in the sense that it is identical with the feeling of pleasure, but that it is *a* pleasure, a source of pleasant feeling. This view of pleasure and pain appears at *Republic* 585 A ff. and was probably widely held in the latter half of the fifth century. A fragment of doxographical tradition[1] ascribes it to Empedocles, though it is unlikely that the actual term ἀναπλήρωσις there used was employed by him. Although Plato in the present passage applies it only to pleasures (and pains) originating in the body, we shall find later that pleasures of purely mental origin also are 'replenishments'.

Socrates   Protarchus

Soc. And now what we must do next is to see in what each of them 31 B is found, and what happens to bring it about that they occur whenever they do. Take pleasure first; we took it first when examining its kind, and we will do the same in the present case. However, we shall never be able properly to examine pleasure apart from pain.

Prot. Well, if that ought to be our line of approach, let us take it.

Soc. Now I wonder if you share my view as regards their occurrence?

Prot. What is your view?   c

Soc. That both pleasure and pain are natural experiences that occur in the 'combined' class.[2]

Prot. Will you remind us, my dear Socrates, which of our previously mentioned classes you allude to by the term 'combined'?

Soc. Really, Protarchus! Well, I'll do my best.

Prot. Thank you.

Soc. Let us understand 'combined' as the third of our four classes.

Prot. The one you spoke of after the Unlimited and the Limit, and in which you put health and harmony,[3] I think, also.

Soc. Perfectly right. Now please give me your most careful D attention.

[1] Diels-Kranz, *Vors.* 31 A95: 'E. τὰς ἡδονὰς γίνεσθαί (sc. φησι) τοῖς μὲν ὁμοίοις ⟨ἐκ⟩ τῶν ὁμοίων, κατὰ δὲ τὸ ἐλλεῖπον πρὸς τὴν ἀναπλήρωσιν, ὥστε τῷ ἐλλείποντι ἡ ὄρεξις τοῦ ὁμοίου.

[2] The sphere, or seat, of the realisation of pleasure and pain is a living organism; and since such an organism is *informed* matter, i.e. a definite and precise structure of material constituents, it may be regarded as an instance of a μεικτόν as previously defined; cf. 32 A τὸ ἐκ τῆς ἀπείρου καὶ πέρατος κατὰ φύσιν ἔμψυχον γεγονὸς εἶδος. There is, of course, no contradiction between this assertion that pleasure and pain are *experienced* in a μεικτόν (ἐν τῷ κοινῷ) and the previous doctrine that they *belong* to the ἄπειρον.

[3] 'Harmony' (which is a legitimate rendering of ἁρμονία in this context) was not in fact amongst the examples of μεικτά at 26 A, but it was implied in the mention of μουσική.

Prot. Continue, please.

Soc. I maintain that, when we find a disturbance of the harmony in a living creature, that is the time at which its natural condition is disturbed and distress therewith occurs.

Prot. That sounds very probable.

Soc. Conversely, when the harmony is being restored and a return is made to its natural condition, we may say that pleasure occurs. I am permitting myself a very brief and rapid statement of a most important fact.

E   *Prot.* I think you are right, Socrates, but let us try to express this same truth even more clearly.

Soc. Well, I suppose commonplace, obvious instances will be the easiest to understand.

Prot. Such as —?

Soc. Hunger, say, is a form of disturbance, of pain, isn't it?

Prot. Yes.

Soc. And eating, as the corresponding restoration, is a form of pleasure?

Prot. Yes.

Soc. Then again thirst is a form of destruction, of pain, whereas
32 the restoration effected by a liquid acting on that which has become dried up is a form of pleasure.[1] Or once again, the unnatural disruption or dissolution brought about by stifling heat is a pain, whereas the coolness which restores us to our natural state is a pleasure.

Prot. Certainly.

Soc. And the disturbance of a creature's natural state consequent on the freezing of its liquids by cold is a pain; while the reverse process, which restores that state when that which is frozen breaks up and returns to its former condition, is a pleasure. Now consider whether this statement is satisfactory, which puts the thing in a general formula:
B when the natural state of a living organism, constituted, as I have maintained, of the Unlimited and the Limit, is destroyed, that destruction is pain; conversely, when such organisms return to their own true nature, this reversion is invariably pleası

Prot. So be it; I think that gives us at least an outline.

---

[1] καὶ λύσις is rightly bracketed by Schleiermacher and Burnet; it is a gloss by someone who failed to see that φθορά corresponds to λύσις in E6. ἡ τοῦ ὑγροῦ δύναμις is a quasi-technical expression, arising from the tendency of physicians to regard 'Hot', 'Cold', 'Moist', etc. from the standpoint of the 'power' which they had in acting on a patient's body. See Cornford, *Plato's Theory of Knowledge*, p. 234 f.

32 B–36 C   *Pleasures of anticipation; the part played in them by
sensation, memory and desire*

A second kind of pleasures and pains are those consisting in anticipation
of the first kind; a long examination of these now follows. The main
purpose is to lead to the conclusion that such pleasures often occur
simultaneously with *actual* present pain, thereby constituting one type
of what are later called 'mixed pleasures'; other types will be afterwards
discerned.

The existence of 'mixed pleasures' is in Plato's mind from the outset,
and one of the main objects of the dialogue is to show that a great many
kinds of pleasure are mixed or impure, and therefore do not merit a
place amongst the ingredients of the Human Good. This first type of
mixed pleasures is discovered by means of a subtle analysis of the
contribution of memory, desire and sensation to the occurrence of
pleasures of anticipation; in the course of which we learn that 'it is to
the soul that all impulse and desire, and indeed the determining principle
of the whole creature belong' (35 D).

It seems likely that, apart from the relevance of this psychological
discussion to the general purpose of the dialogue, Plato wishes to
correct misconceptions which might have arisen in regard to the part
played by body and soul respectively in pleasure and desire. Nothing
indeed in earlier dialogues had warranted a belief that these are bodily
events; yet such statements as that of *Phaedo* 66 C καὶ γὰρ πολέμους καὶ
στάσεις καὶ μάχας οὐδὲν ἄλλο παρέχει ἢ τὸ σῶμα καὶ αἱ τούτου ἐπιθυμίαι,
or *Gorgias* 499 D κατὰ τὸ σῶμα ἅς νυνδὴ ἐλέγομεν ἐν τῷ ἐσθίειν καὶ
πίνειν ἡδονάς, as also the frequent tendency in many dialogues to re-
strict ἡδονή to pleasure of sense, might well have led some astray.

We might have expected Socrates to say, at 35 D, that pleasure and
pain, just as much as desire, are psychical, not bodily events. In point
of fact he does not explicitly[1] say so anywhere in the dialogue, and he
often uses language which appears to imply the opposite: e.g. 45 A
ἆρ' οὖν, αἱ πρόχειροί γε αἵπερ καὶ μέγιστοι τῶν ἡδονῶν, ὃ λέγομεν
πολλάκις, αἱ περὶ τὸ σῶμά εἰσιν αὗται; 46 B εἰσὶ τοίνυν μείξεις (sc.
ἡδονῆς καὶ λύπης) αἱ μὲν κατὰ τὸ σῶμα ἐν αὐτοῖς τοῖς σώμασιν, αἱ δ'
αὐτῆς τῆς ψυχῆς ἐν τῇ ψυχῇ. But this is merely a loose way of expressing the fact that the *source* of the feeling (in the latter passage a mixture
of pleasure and pain) is in the body: cf. 41 C τὸ δὲ τὴν ἀλγηδόνα ἤ τινα
διὰ πάθος ἡδονὴν τὸ σῶμα ἦν τὸ παρεχόμενον. Plato's real belief is
expressed at *Rep.* 584 C, where Socrates speaks of αἱ διὰ τοῦ σώματος
ἐπὶ τὴν ψυχὴν τείνουσαι καὶ λεγόμεναι ἡδοναί. Similarly Aristotle often
allows himself to speak of 'bodily pleasures', e.g. *E.N.* 1104 B 5, 1154 A 8,
but his real doctrine appears unmistakably at 1173 B 7–13.

---

[1] It is however plainly implied at 55 B; see note on p. 112 below.

32 B   *Soc.* Well then, may we take it that one kind of pleasure and pain consists in this pair of experiences?

Prot. We may.

Soc. Now take what the soul itself feels when expecting these c experiences, the pleasant, confident feeling of anticipation that precedes a pleasure, and the apprehensive, distressful feeling that precedes a pain.

Prot. Yes, of course: that is a different kind of pleasure and pain, which belongs to the soul itself, apart from the body, and arises through expectation.

Soc. You grasp what I mean. I think, if I may put my own view, that by taking these two experiences pure and without any admixture of pain in the one case and pleasure in the other—I think that[1] we shall get a clear answer to the question about pleasure, the question whether D everything classed as pleasure is to be welcomed, or whether we ought to grant that to some other of those classes that we previously distinguished, while with pleasure and pain the case stands as with hot and cold and all things like that, namely that sometimes they are to be welcomed and sometimes are not: the reason being that they are not in themselves good, though some of them sometimes and somehow[2] acquire the character of good things.

Prot. You are quite right: that is the proper sort of way to thrash out the subject of our present quest.

Soc. First, then, let us look together into the following point. If E what we are maintaining is really true, if there is distress at the time of deterioration and pleasure at the time of restoration, then let us consider any such creatures as are experiencing neither deterioration nor restoration, and ask what their condition must be at the time in question. Please pay careful attention to what I ask, and tell me: is it not beyond all doubt that at such a time a creature feels neither pleasure nor pain in any degree whatever?

Prot. Yes, it is beyond doubt.

Soc. So this is a third sort of condition that we have, distinct alike 33 from the condition of one who feels pleasure and from that of one who feels pain?

Prot. Certainly.

Soc. Come along then, and do your best to bear it in mind; it will

---

[1] ὡς δοκεῖ at c 7 is probably a mere repetition of κατά γε τὴν ἐμὴν δόξαν.
[2] Reading ὅπῃ for ὅτε with Badham in D 6.

make a big difference as regards our judgment of pleasure whether you do bear it in mind or do not. Now there is a small point in this connexion that we had better settle, if you please.

Prot. Tell me what it is.

Soc. You know that for one who has chosen[1] the life of intelligence there is nothing to prevent him living in this fashion.

Prot. A life, you mean, of neither pleasure nor pain?   B

Soc. Yes, for when we were comparing the lives just now we said, I believe, that for one who had chosen the life of reason and intelligence there must be no experiencing of any pleasure, great or small.

Prot. That was certainly what we said.

Soc. Then he at all events has it in his power to live after this fashion;[2] and perhaps it is not a wild surmise that this is of all lives the most godlike.

Prot. Certainly it is not to be supposed that the gods feel either pleasure or its opposite.

Soc. No, of course it is not: it would be unseemly for either feeling to arise in them. But to that question we will give further consideration later on, if it should be relevant, and we will set down the point to the score of Intelligence in the competition for second prize, if we cannot c do so in the competition for the first.

Prot. Quite right.

Soc. Now to continue: pleasure of this second kind, which belongs, as we said, to the soul alone, always involves memory.

Prot. How so?

Soc. I fancy that we must first take up the enquiry what memory is, or perhaps even, before memory, what sensation is, if we mean to get properly clear about these matters.

Prot. What do you mean?   D

Soc. You must take it that amongst the experiences that are constantly affecting our bodies some are exhausted in the body before passing through to the soul, thus leaving the latter unaffected, while others penetrate both body and soul and set up a sort of disturbance which is both peculiar to each and common to both.[3]

[1] I retain τῷ and ἑλομένῳ in A 8. The abnormal datives, both here and in B 3–4, are due to the need of avoiding the collocation τὸν τὸν τοῦ.

[2] The inconsistency with 22 A is only apparent: for we are meant to understand that it is only a god that could choose this life.

[3] κοινόν seems to contradict ἴδιον, but the meaning is that whereas the body (i.e. the sense-organ) suffers a literal 'shaking', the soul or consciousness, not being an extended magnitude, can only be shaken figuratively. Hence the common σεισμός is differentiated into two modes.

Prot. Let us take it to be so.

Soc. Now shall we be right if we say that those which do not penetrate both are undetected by the soul, while those which do penetrate both are not undetected thereby?

E *Prot.* Of course.

Soc. You must not suppose that by 'being undetected' I mean that a process of forgetting is involved; forgetting is the passing away of memory, whereas in the case we are discussing memory has not as yet come to be; and it would be absurd to talk of the loss of what does not exist and never has existed, would it not?

Prot. Of course.

Soc. Then just alter the names.

Prot. How?

Soc. Instead of speaking, as you now do,[1] of 'forgetting' what is undetected by the soul when it is unaffected by the disturbances of the 34 body, you must substitute the term 'non-sensation'.

Prot. I understand.

Soc. And if you apply to that movement, which occurs when soul and body come together in a single affection and are moved both together, the term 'sensation', you will be expressing yourself properly.

Prot. Very true.

Soc. Then we understand already what we mean by sensation.

Prot. Certainly.

Soc. Memory it would, in my opinion, be right to call the preservation of sensation.

B *Prot.* Quite so.

Soc. Then by 'recollection' we mean, do we not, something different from memory?

Prot. I suppose so.

Soc. I will suggest the point of difference.

Prot. What is it?

Soc. When that which has been experienced by the soul in common with the body is recaptured, so far as may be, by and in the soul itself apart from the body, then we speak of 'recollecting' something. Is that not so?

Prot. Undoubtedly.

[1] Protarchus has not, in fact, used the word 'forgetting' (λήθη): but Socrates means that he, and people in general, would be likely to be misled by the connexion of the Greek verb λανθάνειν (λεληθέναι) 'to escape the notice of' with the corresponding noun λήθη 'forgetting'. The Greek for 'to forget' is ἐπιλανθάνεσθαι.

Soc. And further, when the soul that has lost the memory of a sensation or of what it has learnt resumes that memory within itself and goes over the old ground, we regularly speak of these processes as 'recollections'.[1]   c

Prot. I agree.

Soc. And now I will tell you the point of all we have been saying.

Prot. What is it?

Soc. To get the clearest notion that we possibly can of the pleasure of soul apart from body, and of desire as well. I think that the procedure we are adopting promises to explain them both.

Prot. Let us proceed then, Socrates.

Soc. Our examination will necessarily, I think, involve saying a good deal about the origin of pleasure and the various shapes it takes. And D in point of fact it seems necessary to preface that with an understanding of the nature of desire and the seat of its occurrence.

Prot. Then let us examine that; we shan't be the losers.

Soc. O yes we shall, Protarchus, and I'll tell you of what; if we find what we are now looking for, we shall be the losers of the very perplexity that now besets us.

Prot. A good retort! Then let us try to deal with our next point.

Soc. Were we not saying just now that hunger, thirst, and so on and so forth, are desires[2] of some sort?   E

Prot. Unquestionably.

Soc. What was the identical feature, then, that we had in view that makes us call such widely different things[3] by one name?

Prot. Upon my word, Socrates, I'm afraid it is not easy to answer that; still, answer it we must.

Soc. Then let us go back to where we were and start afresh.

Prot. Go back where?

Soc. We talk commonly, do we not, of a man 'having a thirst'?

Prot. Certainly.

Soc. Meaning that he is becoming empty?

Prot. Of course.

Soc. Then is his thirst a desire?

---

[1] The words καὶ μνήμας must either be excised (Gloël, Burnet) or replaced by something like καὶ ἀναλήψεις μνήμης (Bury).

[2] This is a slip: they were mentioned at 31 E but were not said to be desires. The slip is, however, unimportant, for plainly they are desires.

[3] It would be unnatural to call hunger and thirst 'widely different'; but amongst the πολλὰ ἕτερα τοιαῦτα is included the lack of warmth and coolness spoken of at 32 A, as well as deficiencies in respect of other bodily requirements.

Prot. Yes, a desire for drink.

35   *Soc.* For drink, or for a replenishment by drink?

Prot. For a replenishment, I should think.

Soc. When one becomes empty then, apparently he desires the opposite of what he is experiencing: being emptied, he longs to be filled.

Prot. Obviously.

Soc. Well now, is it possible that one who is emptied for the first time could apprehend replenishment whether by means of a perception or a memory, replenishment being something that he is neither experiencing in the present nor has ever experienced in the past?

Prot. Of course not.

B   *Soc.* Nevertheless we must admit that one who desires, desires something.

Prot. Yes, of course.

Soc. Then it is not what he is experiencing that he desires; for he is thirsty, and thirst is an emptying, whereas what he desires is replenishment.

Prot. Yes.

Soc. Then there must be something in the make-up of a thirsty man which apprehends replenishment.

Prot. Necessarily.

Soc. And it cannot be the body, for that of course is being emptied.

Prot. No.

Soc. Hence the only alternative is that the soul apprehends the
c replenishment, and does so obviously through memory. For through what else could it do so?[1]

---

[1] At first sight Socrates seems to contradict here what he has said at 35 A 6–9, viz. that on the first occasion of κένωσις there can be no memory of πλήρωσις: and this contradiction Apelt (note 53 to his translation of the dialogue) seeks to remove by understanding the memory of 35 C 1 to be not of πλήρωσις but of original equilibrium. This I find difficult to accept. For if Plato meant it he is guilty of an incredible negligence of expression; how can the reader fail to take the almost immediately preceding genitive τῆς πληρώσεως to be the genitive implied in τῇ μνήμῃ? But though Apelt has given (as I think) the wrong solution, he seems to see, as nobody else does, that there is a problem, and it may therefore be helpful to transcribe his note before I offer my own solution.

'Dieser Nachweis von der rein geistigen Natur auch der körperlichen Lust ist ungemein interessant und, wie schon bemerkt, besonders wichtig. Es fragt sich nur, was Platon unter der Erinnerung versteht, auf der nach ihm all diese Lust beruht. Er weist 35 A ausdrücklich den Gedanken zurück, dass derjenige, der zum erstenmal durstet, auf Grund der Erinnerung auf die Füllung bedacht sein könne, denn diese Füllung habe er ja an sich noch nie erfahren. Also woran erinnert er sich? Nicht an die Füllung, wohl aber an jenen ursprünglichen Gleichgewichtzustand, den Platon als Ausgangspunkt aller sinnlichen Lust und Unlust

Prot. It's hard to point to anything else.

Soc. Then do we realise what has emerged from this discussion?

Prot. What?

Soc. It has told us that desire does not belong to the body.

Prot. How so?

Soc. Because it has revealed that the effort of every creature is opposed to that which its body is experiencing.

Prot. Quite so.

Soc. Moreover, the fact that impulse leads the creature in a direction opposite to its experience proves, I fancy, the existence of a memory of something opposite to that experience.

Prot. Undoubtedly.

Soc. Our discussion then, inasmuch as it has proved that memory D is what leads us on to the objects of our desire, has made it plain that it is to the soul that all impulse and desire, and indeed the determining principle of the whole creature, belong.

Prot. You are perfectly right.

Soc. Then there can be no gainsaying that our bodies cannot possibly feel thirst or hunger or anything of that sort?

Prot. Very true.

Soc. Now here is a further point that calls for our remark in this same connexion. It seems to me that our argument aims at revealing a certain sort of life amidst these very things we have been speaking of.

annimmt und den er eben deshalb wiederholt mit so grossen Nachdruck betont....'

I believe that the clue to the argument is what Socrates does not actually say, but only implies: viz. that no desire (ἐπιθυμία) can occur on the first occasion of κένωσις. There is a strong contrast between ὁ τὸ πρῶτον κενούμενος (A 6) and ἀλλὰ μὴν ὁ γε ἐπιθυμῶν (B 1): and it is just this contrast that is intended to carry the implication in question. Accordingly I paraphrase the argument as follows:

It might be supposed that, since thirst (which is an ἐπιθυμία, 34 E 13) occurs when the physical organism is 'depleted', it is the body that ἐπιθυμεῖ. But if that were so, desire would occur at the first κένωσις; yet it does not, for desire involves the notion or 'apprehension' (ἐφάπτεσθαι) of something *opposite* to the physical experience of κένωσις, the notion namely of πλήρωσις; and this notion, just because it is an opposite notion to anything that the body can, at the first κένωσις (i.e. before any πλήρωσις has been experienced), possibly possess, must belong to soul. In short, desire involves a preceding bodily πλήρωσις, of which the soul conceives the notion by way of memory.

The words κενοῦται γάρ που at B 9 do not mean that the reason why it is impossible for the body ἐφάπτεσθαι πληρώσεως is that the same thing cannot ἐφάπτεσθαι two opposites simultaneously, as Taylor supposes; if they did, there would, so far as I can see, be no point in introducing the topic of the *first* κένωσις at all; rather they mean that, the only relevant experience of the body hitherto being that of κένωσις (which it is at the moment in question experiencing), it cannot be conceived as apprehending πλήρωσις.

E *Prot.* What things? What kind of life are you speaking of?

Soc. The processes of replenishment and being emptied, in fact all processes concerned with the preservation or decay of living beings; and our alternating feelings of distress and pleasure, according as we pass from one of these processes to the other.

Prot. Quite so.

Soc. And what about such times as we are in an intermediate state?

Prot. Intermediate?

Soc. When we feel distress by reason of what we are experiencing, and at the same time remember the pleasures whose occurrence would relieve our distress, though the replenishment in question is still in the
36 future. How do we stand then? May we say that we are in an intermediate state, or may we not?

Prot. By all means.

Soc. And is the state as a whole one of distress or of pleasure?

Prot. Pleasure! No, indeed: rather a state of twofold pain, pain of the body in respect of its actual experience, and pain of the soul in respect of an unsatisfied expectation.

Soc. What makes you call it twofold pain, Protarchus? Is it not the case that sometimes the emptying process is associated with a distinct
B hope of coming replenishment, while at other times there is no such hope?

Prot. Yes, of course.

Soc. Then don't you think that when hoping for replenishment we feel pleasure through what we remember, though nevertheless we feel pain simultaneously because of the emptying process going on at the times in question?[1]

Prot. Yes, no doubt.

Soc. At such a time then men, and animals too, feel both pain and pleasure at once.

Prot. It looks like it.

Soc. Now take the case when we are being emptied and have no hope of attaining replenishment. Is not it then that there occurs that twofold feeling of pain which you descried just now, though you
C thought the pain to be 'simply double', drawing no distinctions?

Prot. Very true, Socrates.

[1] There seems no need to bracket τοῖς χρόνοις; cf. 50 A.

36 C–38 A *True and false pleasures*

We have just seen that, when actual pain of depletion is not accompanied by any hope of pleasure of replenishment, there is a condition of twofold pain; but when it is so accompanied we seem to be pleased and pained simultaneously. This at once raises the question of the truth or falsity of such pleasures and pains. Can either the pleasure or the pain be true, if it is accompanied by its opposite? It is a big question (λόγον οὐ πάνυ σμικρόν, 36 D), and will dominate the rest of the dialogue.

Socrates begins by stating Protarchus's position as this, that whatever our condition, sane or insane, waking or dreaming, it is impossible for us to *suppose* that we are pleased or pained without really being so. Protarchus agrees that this is his own and everyone's view. Let us then examine it. Opinion, whether right or wrong, is always 'really' (ὄντως) opinion: therefore presumably pleasure, whether right or wrong, is always 'really' pleasure. On what grounds then can we maintain that, whereas opinions differ *qua* true and false, pleasures do not?

The first suggestion made is that pleasures admit of various qualities, great, small, intense, bad. May they not then have the quality of 'rightness' (ὀρθότης)? Just as we call an opinion 'not right' if it makes a mistake about the object opined, so we shall call a pleasure (or pain) 'not right' if it involves a mistake about the object at which it is felt (περὶ τὸ ἐφ' ᾧ λυπεῖται ἢ τοὐναντίον ἁμαρτάνουσαν, 37 E).

The point here made is this, that to abstract the mere pleasure-feeling from its objective reference, to consider it out of relation to its object, is just as untrue to fact as it would be to abstract the mere act of opining or judging from *its* object. The indubitable fact that Pleasure is always really Pleasure is no ground for denying that an actual pleasure, just as much as an actual opinion, may be wrong or mistaken. Only by an unreal abstraction can either be divorced from its object, that *about which* we opine (judge) or are pleased.

Protarchus however does not grasp this; his view is that the 'mistakenness' is something lying outside the pleasure, a wrong opinion held concurrently with the feeling; hence he still denies that any pleasure can in itself be called false. Plato no doubt hopes that his readers will be more understanding than Protarchus; but to convince his interlocutor Socrates must go deeper into the problem.

It should be realised that the present section does not overthrow Protarchus' contention, shared as he says by everybody, that we cannot suppose we are pleased or pained without really being so. Whether this is or is not the case is still left open. All that is so far maintained is that a pleasure (or pain) may quite well be false without ceasing to be a pleasure (or pain). Falsity is not the same thing as non-existence.

Socrates   Protarchus

36c **Soc.** Now let me suggest a use to which we may put our examination of these experiences.

Prot. What is it?

Soc. Shall we say that these pains and pleasures are true or false? Or that some are true, and others not?

Prot. But how, Socrates, can pleasures or pains be false?

Soc. How can fears be true or false, Protarchus? Or expectations, or opinions?

D   **Prot.** For myself, I should be inclined to allow it in the case of opinions, but not in the other cases.

Soc. What's that? It really looks as if we were raising a question of no small magnitude.

Prot. That is true.

Soc. But is it relevant to what has preceded? Philebus the younger should ask himself that question.[1]

Prot. That question perhaps, yes.

Soc. Anyhow, we ought to have nothing to do with extraneous disquisitions, or with anything in the way of irrelevant discussion.

Prot. You are right.

E   **Soc.** Now tell me this. I have felt curious ever so long about these same problems that we raised just now. What do you maintain? Are there not false, as opposed to true, pleasures?

Prot. How could that be?

Soc. Then, according to you, no one, be he dreaming or waking, or insane or deranged, ever thinks that he feels pleasure but does not really feel it, or thinks he feels pain, but does not really feel it.

Prot. All of us, Socrates, regard all that as holding good.

Soc. Well, are you right? Ought we not to consider whether what you say is right or wrong?

Prot. I think we ought.

37   **Soc.** Then let us state in even plainer terms what you were just now saying about pleasure and opinion. There is such a thing, I imagine, as holding an opinion?

Prot. Yes.

Soc. And as feeling a pleasure?

Prot. Yes.

---

[1] As 'Philebus the elder' had asked it at 18 A.

Soc. Is there also that about which the opinion is held?

Prot. Of course.

Soc. And that in which the pleasure is felt?

Prot. Undoubtedly.

Soc. Then the subject holding an opinion, whether it be rightly or wrongly held, is always in the position of really holding an opinion?

Prot. Of course.

Soc. And similarly the subject feeling pleasure, whether it be rightly or wrongly felt, will obviously be always in the position of really feeling a pleasure?

Prot. Yes, that is so too.

Soc. The question then must be faced, how it is that whereas we commonly find opinion both true and false, pleasure is true only, and that though in respect of reality holding an opinion and feeling a pleasure are on the same footing.

Prot. Yes, that question must be faced.

Soc. Is the point this, do you think, that in the case of opinion falsehood and truth supervene, with the result that it becomes not merely an opinion but a certain sort of opinion, true or false respectively? c

Prot. Yes.

Soc. But then we have got a further question on which we must come to an agreement, namely whether it is at all possible that, as against other things that have quality, pleasure and pain never have qualities but are simply what they are.

Prot. Clearly so.

Soc. But in point of fact it is easy to see that actually they do have qualities: we spoke a while ago of their being great, small, and intense, pains and pleasures alike.

Prot. To be sure we did. D

Soc. And what's more, Protarchus, if badness is added to any of the things in question, shall we not say that it thereby becomes a bad opinion, and similarly a bad pleasure?

Prot. Why, of course, Socrates.

Soc. Once again, if rightness or its opposite is added to any of them, presumably we shall say that an opinion, if it has rightness, is right, and the same with a pleasure?

Prot. Necessarily.

Soc. But if the content of an opinion that is held be mistaken, then E must we not agree that the opinion, inasmuch as it is making a mistake, is not right, not opining rightly?

Prot. No, it cannot be.

Soc. Well then, if we observe a pain or a pleasure making a mistake in regard to the object arousing the respective feelings, shall we attach to it any term of commendation such as 'right' or 'sound'?

Prot. Impossible, if the pleasure is *ex hypothesi* mistaken.

Soc. Now look here; I fancy we often experience pleasure in association with an opinion that is not right, but false.

38   *Prot.* Of course; and then, that being so, Socrates, we call the opinion false, but the pleasure itself nobody could ever term false.

Soc. Well, Protarchus, you are putting up a gallant defence of the cause of pleasure by what you say now.

Prot. O no, I am merely repeating what I have heard.

38 A–40 E   *The connexion between False Judgment and False Pleasure*

Protarchus has denied that there can be false or mistaken pleasures in any other sense than that a pleasure can be associated with a false judgment. This position is now met by a careful analysis of the origin of judgment and pleasure and of their connexion: its result is to show that although the quality of a pleasure as true or false does indeed depend (in the case of some pleasures, at least) on the quality of the judgment, yet the pleasure itself has that quality. Socrates states this conclusion quite clearly, when he looks back at this section a little later on, at 42 A: judgments, according as they are false or true, 'infect' the pains and pleasures with what they have 'caught' themselves (τότε μὲν αἱ δόξαι ψευδεῖς τε καὶ ἀληθεῖς αὗται γιγνόμεναι τὰς λύπας τε καὶ ἡδονὰς ἅμα τοῦ παρ' αὐταῖς παθήματος ἀνεπίμπλασαν).

Judgment is the joint product of sense-perception, memory, and certain unspecified feelings or emotions (παθήματα, 39 A) associated therewith; by these παθήματα Plato probably means us to understand fear, confidence, anger, love, and others. False judgment is traced to indistinctness of sense-perception, though we need not suppose that Plato is here giving an exhaustive account of error, a problem dealt with at greater length in the *Theaetetus* and *Sophist*.

The formation of a judgment is graphically represented as a 'writing of statements' (λόγοι) in our minds by a scribe, who symbolises the complex of sense-perception, memory and emotion; but between this and the occurrence of pleasure Plato interpolates the mental picture (εἰκών), the work of a painter (ʒωγράφος, 39 B), who symbolises the faculty which Aristotle calls φαντασία, imagination or image-making; Plato himself later uses the word φαντάσματα (40 A) as a synonym for εἰκόνες. These pictures, which, like judgments, may be of the past, present or future, correspond with reality, or fail to correspond, according as the judgments on which they follow are true or false; and if the picture is of something which would please us if we really had it, e.g. gold, pleasure follows. 'People often have visions of securing great quantities of gold, which brings them pleasure upon pleasure; indeed they behold themselves in the picture immensely delighted with themselves' (40 A).

Our attention is mainly concentrated on false *future* pleasures such as this; but besides the pleasant anticipation of an unreal future we may also have the pleasant reminiscence of an unreal past, or the pleasant illusion of an unreal present.

Incidentally it is suggested (40 B–C) that false pleasures of this kind are bad in a moral sense: good men, being dear to the gods, have true statements and pictures in their minds, evil men false ones. This in itself implies that the account of the origin of error here given cannot be complete: there must be other kinds of false judgment than that due to indistinct sense-perception. Plato is doubtless hinting at false value-judgments, which spring not from the weakness of our bodily eyes but from the blindness of our spiritual vision. The man who is θεοφιλής, and therefore blessed with true judgment, is one who like Socrates himself has followed after God by 'tending his own soul' so as to heal himself of spiritual blindness

Socrates   Protarchus

Soc. But do we find no difference, my friend, between a pleasure 38A associated with right opinion and knowledge and one associated, as is constantly happening to every one of us, with false opinion and ignorance?

Prot. I should say they differ considerably.   B

Soc. Then let us proceed to contemplate the difference.

Prot. Pray take the road on which you descry it.

Soc. Very well, I will take you along this one.

Prot. Yes?

Soc. Opinion, we agree, is sometimes false, sometimes true?

Prot. That is so.

Soc. And, as we said just now, pleasure and pain frequently accompany these true and false opinions.

Prot. Quite so.

Soc. Now is it not always memory and perception that give rise to opinion and to the attempts we make to reach a judgment?

Prot. Certainly.   C

Soc. Let me suggest what we must believe to occur in this connexion.

Prot. Well?

Soc. If a man sees objects that come into his view from a distance and indistinctly, would you agree that he commonly wants to decide about what he sees?

Prot. I should.

Soc. Then the next step will be that he puts a question to himself.

Prot. What question?

Soc. 'What is that object which catches my eye there beside the D rock under a tree?' Don't you think that is what he would say to himself, if he had caught sight of some appearance of the sort?

Prot. Of course.

Soc. And then he would answer his own question and say, if he got it right, 'It is a man.'

Prot. Certainly.

Soc. Or again, if he went astray and thought what he was looking at was something made by shepherds, he might very likely call it an image.

Prot. He might, quite well.

E *Soc.* And if he had someone with him, he would put what he said to himself into actual speech addressed to his companion, audibly uttering those same thoughts, so that what before we called opinion has now become assertion.

Prot. Of course.

Soc. Whereas if he is alone he continues thinking the same thing by himself, going on his way maybe for a considerable time with the thought in his mind.

Prot. Undoubtedly.

Soc. Well now, I wonder whether you share my view on these matters.

Prot. What is it?

Soc. It seems to me that at such times our soul is like a book.

Prot. How so?

39 *Soc.* It appears to me that the conjunction of memory with sensations, together with the feelings consequent upon memory and sensation, may be said as it were to write words in our souls; and when this experience writes what is true, the result is that true opinion and true assertions spring up in us; while when the internal scribe that

I have suggested writes what is false we get the opposite sort of opinions and assertions.[1]

Prot. That certainly seems to me right, and I approve of the way B you put it.

Soc. Then please give your approval to the presence of a second artist in our souls at such a time.

Prot. Who is that?

Soc. A painter, who comes after the writer and paints in the soul pictures of these assertions that we make.

Prot. How do we make out that he in his turn acts, and when?

Soc. When we have got those opinions and assertions clear of the act of sight, or other sense, and as it were see in ourselves pictures or C images of what we previously opined or asserted. That does happen with us, doesn't it?

Prot. Indeed it does.

Soc. Then are the pictures of true opinions and assertions true, and the pictures of false ones false?

Prot. Unquestionably.

Soc. Well, if we are right so far, here is one more point in this connexion for us to consider.

Prot. What is that?

Soc. Does all this necessarily befall us in respect of the present and the past, but not in respect of the future?

Prot. On the contrary, it applies equally to them all.

Soc. We said previously, did we not, that pleasures and pains felt D in the soul alone might precede those that come through the body? That must mean that we have anticipatory pleasures and anticipatory pains in regard to the future.[2]

[1] The text of this difficult sentence is, I think, successfully defended by Stallbaum and Friedländer. The 'scribe' is a being composite of present sensation, memory, and the παθήματα (fear, confidence, anger, etc.) consequent upon the conjunction of sensation with memory. As composite he passes from plural to singular in the words τοῦτο τὸ πάθημα in A 4, which should not be bracketed.

[2] This appeal to the previously established fact of pleasures and pains of anticipation which belong to the soul alone, apart from the body (32 C), is intended to prove that the judgments and images with which pleasure and pain are connected are not in all cases based on sense-experience, but may be 'free', that is to say the work of the mind by itself. To take the illustration given a little later (40 A), the man who derives great pleasure from the vision of abundant wealth coming to him is not judging about present or past experience, nor is his mental image the stored product of experience: his mind is making 'statements' and painting 'pictures' of the future simply by itself. Plato's account seems perfectly correct in so far as it asserts that the pleasure derived from hope (and the pain derived from fear) involve judgment and imagination just as much as the pleasure and pain occasioned by sense-experience.

Prot. Very true.

Soc. Now do those writings and paintings, which a while ago we
E assumed to occur within ourselves, apply to past and present only, and
not to the future?

Prot. Indeed they do.

Soc. When you say 'indeed they do', do you mean that the last
sort are all expectations concerned with what is to come, and that we
are full of expectations all our life long?

Prot. Undoubtedly.

Soc. Well now, here is a further question for you to answer.

Prot. Yes?

Soc. Isn't a man who is just, pious, and in every way good dear to
the gods?

Prot. To be sure.

Soc. And may not the opposite be said of one who is unjust and
40 altogether bad?

Prot. Of course.

Soc. But every human being, as we said just now, is full of expectations?

Prot. Certainly.

Soc. But what we call expectations are in fact assertions that each
of us makes to himself.

Prot. Yes.

Soc. To which must be added the representations produced[1] by our
painter. People often have visions of securing great quantities of gold,
and pleasure upon pleasure in consequence; indeed they behold themselves in the picture immensely delighted with themselves.

B   *Prot.* I know.

Soc. Now may we say that what is written in the minds of the good
is as a rule a true communication, since they are dear to the gods,
while with the evil the opposite as a rule is the case? What do you
think?

Prot. Certainly we should say so.

Soc. So the evil, no less than the good, have pleasures painted in
their minds, but these pleasures, I imagine, are false.

Prot. Of course.

---

[1] τὰ φαντάσματα ⟨τὰ⟩ ἐзωγραφημένα (Bury) seems necessary in A 9. Ἐλπίς involves the work of the painter as well as that of the scribe, 'imagination' as well
as judgment (opinion).

Soc. Bad men, then, delight for the most part in false pleasures, good c men in true ones.

Prot. Inevitably so.

Soc. Hence we reach the result that false pleasures do exist in men's souls, being really a rather ridiculous imitation of true pleasures; and the same applies to pains.

Prot. Yes, they do exist.

Soc. Now we found that, though a person holding any opinion at all must hold it in fact, yet it might sometimes have reference to what was not a fact, either of the present, the past, or the future.

Prot. Quite so.

Soc. And there, I think, lay the source of our false opinion, of our D holding opinions falsely. Did it not?

Prot. Yes.

Soc. Well then, should we not ascribe a corresponding condition, as regards these references,[1] to pains and pleasures?

Prot. How do you mean?

Soc. I mean that though anyone who feels pleasure at all, no matter how groundless it be, always really feels that pleasure, yet sometimes it has no reference to any present or past fact, while in many cases, perhaps in most, it has reference to what never will be a fact.

Prot. That too must be so, Socrates. E

40 E–42 C   *A second type of false pleasures, due to error in respect*
of hedonic magnitude

The first kind of falsity in pleasures was seen to be due to the transference to the pleasure of the falsity in the judgment, and in the subsequent mental image, on which it ensued; the judgment is described, in a reference back to the previous section at 42 A, as 'infecting' the pleasure with its own characteristic. Such pleasures are false themselves: their falsity does not, as Protarchus believed, lie wholly outside them, in the judgments; pleasure in τὸ μὴ ὄν is itself necessarily false.

In the second type, to which we now come, the falsity attaches even more closely to the pleasures. It arises from what may be called an illusion in respect of hedonic magnitude. Our estimate of the magnitude of a pleasure is often falsified by our setting beside it a simultaneous pain; for pleasure and pain, as we have already learnt, can occur simultaneously; both feelings are of course in the mind; but one is 'supplied' by the body (τὸ σῶμα ἦν τὸ παρεχόμενον, 41 C), while the

---

[1] τούτων in D 5 = τῶν δοξῶν, and ἐν ἐκείνοις denotes the references to present, past, and future reality mentioned at c 9.

other has its source in the mind itself. But since the one is 'seen from a distance' and the other 'seen close at hand'—in other words, since the one is a mental anticipation (of pleasure or pain) and the other an actually present pleasure or pain—we are liable to exaggerate the present feeling and underrate the anticipation-feeling. Moreover, when what *was* an anticipation-feeling has become a present feeling its magnitude appears to have increased relatively to what *was* previously a present pleasure or pain. In all these cases we may say that *part* of the feeling is 'apparent, not real' (φαινόμενον ἀλλ' οὐκ ὄν, 42 B): its real magnitude could only be found by subtracting this illusory part, a feat impossible of achievement. Such falsity of estimate is due to the 'unlimited' nature of pleasure and pain, which we have already noticed (31 A); if pleasure admitted of precise mathematical determination we should not make these mistakes; they are of the same sort as the false guesses at temperature that might be made by a man getting alternately into a hot bath and a cold one before the days of thermometers.

If the reader is inclined to object that what Plato shows here is not that the pleasure itself is false, or partly false, but only that the con-current judgment or estimate of its magnitude is so, he should realize that, in Plato's view at least, this estimate is part and parcel of the pleasure as experienced. Just as we may say 'this bath *feels* very (or rather) hot', so we say 'this experience *feels* very pleasant', 'that experience *felt* rather pleasant'.

A difficulty arises in the passage (41 C) where Plato is establishing the fact of simultaneous, juxtaposed. pleasure and pain. He deduces this from the previous account of desire (ἐπιθυμία), in which we saw that the soul or mind desires the opposite (πλήρωσις) of that which the body is experiencing (κένωσις). But when Socrates says, at 41 C 5–7, 'It was the soul that desired a condition opposite to that of the body, and it was the body that caused our distress, *or our pleasure*, because of the way it was affected', he must mean that there are cases of desire when the body is providing pleasure. What we desire then cannot be anything but the πλήρωσις of the mind itself, namely the pleasure of acquiring knowledge, of which we shall hear later (52 A). Plato cannot say everything at once, as we have remarked before; but the implied reference to these mental pleasures is somewhat troublesome and un-necessary here, since his point about the juxtaposition of pain and pleasure could be quite adequately made without it. The text of the words ἤ τινα διὰ πάθος ἡδονήν has been suspected (see Bury's note), but I have little doubt that it is correct, though we could have wished the words away.

Socrates   Protarchus

40 E   *Soc.* Now will not the same principle hold good in respect of fear, anger, and all such feelings, namely that all of them are sometimes false?

Prot. Assuredly.

Soc. Tell me now, can we distinguish bad opinions from good in any other respect than their falsity?

Prot. No.

Soc. Then neither can we detect any other sense in which pleasures are bad, save in that they are false.

Prot. No, Socrates, what you say is just the opposite of the truth. 41 Surely it is not at all because they are false that we set down pains and pleasures as bad, but because they involve some serious and considerable badness of another sort.

Soc. Well, these bad pleasures whose character is due to badness we will speak of a little later on, if we still think fit to do so.[1] We must, however, discuss those false pleasures—and they are numerous and frequent—which exist or come to exist in us in another way.[2] Maybe we shall find this useful for the decisions we have to make.   B

Prot. Yes, of course, if there are any.

Soc. Well, Protarchus, as I see it, there are. But of course we must not allow this belief[3] to go unexamined until we have got it established.

Prot. Very good.

Soc. Then let us take up our positions for this next round in the argument.

Prot. On we go.

Soc. Well now, we said a while back, if our memory is correct, that when we have within us what we call 'desires', the body stands aloof c from the soul and parts company with it in respect of its affections.

Prot. Our memory is correct: we did say so.

Soc. It was the soul, was it not, that desired a condition opposite to that of the body, and it was the body that caused our distress,[4] or our pleasure, because of the way it was affected?

Prot. It was.

Soc. Then draw the inference in regard to what is happening.

Prot. Tell me.

---

[1] This half-promise is not fulfilled, save in so far as 'pleasures that always go with folly and all other manner of evil' are refused admission into the Mixed Life at 63 E.

[2] κατ' ἄλλον τρόπον in A 7 must be taken with the participles, not (as Apelt) with λεκτέον. Socrates is passing from the falsity of pleasure due to its connexion with false opinion to the falsity of pleasure *per se*.

[3] τοῦτο τὸ δόγμα in B 5 means 'this belief of mine', viz. that there are pleasures false *per se*, which Protarchus has queried in his εἴπερ γε εἰσίν above.

[4] It is still not said, in so many words, that pain and pleasure occur in the soul, not in the body; but the use of παρεχόμενον implies this; the body only originates, or brings about, the psychical experience.

D   *Soc.* Well, what happens at such a time is this: pains and pleasures
exist side by side; opposite as they are, we experience them simultaneously, one beside the other, as appeared just now.[1]

Prot. It appears so, certainly.

Soc. There is a further point that we have mentioned and agreed
upon already as established, is there not?

Prot. What is that?

Soc. That pain and pleasure, both of them, admit of the more and
the less, that is they belong to what is unlimited.

Prot. We did say so. What then?

Soc. What means have we of getting a right decision about these
things?[2]

E   *Prot.* Decision? In what sense do you mean?

Soc. I mean that[3] our resolve to get a decision in these matters
regularly takes some such form as seeking to determine the comparative
magnitude, or degree, or intensity, of a pain and a pleasure, or of one
pain or pleasure as against another.

Prot. Yes, those are the kind of questions: that is what we want to
decide.

Soc. Well now, if it is true that, in the case of vision, to observe
42   magnitudes[4] from a distance and from close at hand obscures the truth
and engenders false judgment, does not the same hold good in the case
of pains and pleasures?

Prot. .Yes, Socrates, and to a much greater degree.

Soc. So here we have the reverse of what we spoke of a little while
ago.[5]

Prot. Have we? How?

Soc. Just now it was the falsity or truth of those opinions that
infected the pains and pleasures with what they had caught themselves.

B   *Prot.* Very true.

Soc. But now the reason why pleasures appear greater and more
intense when compared with something painful, or again, in the reverse

---

[1] At 36 A–B, from which it is clear that of the juxtaposed feelings one or the
other must be a pleasure or pain of anticipation.

[2] ταῦτα (D 11) means 'things that admit of more and less'.

[3] Reading ἢ for εἰ (with Badham) in E 2. Cf. *Rep.* 510 B.

[4] τὰ μεγέθη probably means two or more different magnitudes: the false
judgment arises from seeing one at a great distance and another at a small.

[5] In the last section (38 A–40 E), as explained in τότε μὲν... ἀνεπίμπλασαν below.
The present type of false pleasure may be called the reverse, inasmuch as the false
judgment depends on an illusory feeling.

case, pains appear so by being compared with pleasures, is found in the pleasures and pains *per se*, according as we pass from a distant to a close observation of them, and set them beside one another.

Prot. The reason for what you describe must necessarily be as you say.

Soc. Then if you subtract from each that unreal and only apparent excess which makes them look respectively greater or smaller than they really are, you will acknowledge the subtracted portion to be an incorrect appearance, and you will refrain from asserting that such c pleasure or pain as is felt in respect of that portion[1] is correct and true.

Prot. Yes indeed.

42 C–44 A   *A third type of false pleasures and pains, due to non-recognition of a neutral condition*

If pain occurs when the natural state of an organism is being impaired, and pleasure when it is being restored, there must be a neutral condition, neither pleasurable nor painful, when neither process is taking place. Or if it be contended, as the Heracliteans would contend, that one or the other process must always be taking place, at all events we are often not conscious of it. It is in fact only when the processes are of some magnitude or intensity that we are conscious of them, and feel pleasure or pain: at other times our feeling is neutral. But this neutral feeling, and the 'middle life' corresponding to it, are often wrongly declared to be pleasurable, or again painful.

It is important to realise that this third case differs in an important respect from the two others. In both of those there was a real pleasure or pain, containing an element of falsity; but now there is no ὄντως ἥδεσθαι or λυπεῖσθαι, no real pleasure or pain; this case is not covered by the formula of 37 B, τὸ ἡδόμενον ἄντε ὀρθῶς ἄντε μὴ ὀρθῶς ἥδηται, τό γε ὄντως ἥδεσθαι δῆλον ὡς οὐδέποτ' ἀπολεῖ. On the contrary, we have what Protarchus 'and everybody else' had asserted to be impossible, the case when a man δοκεῖ μὲν χαίρειν, χαίρει δὲ οὐδαμῶς, and δοκεῖ μὲν λυπεῖσθαι, λυπεῖται δ' οὔ.

Ought this false belief that we are experiencing pleasure to be called false pleasure? Logically it ought not: if a certain feeling is not a pleasure at all, it cannot be a qualified pleasure. But Plato does not

---

[1] The expression τὸ ἐπὶ τούτῳ μέρος τῆς ἡδονῆς καὶ λύπης γιγνόμενον is strictly illogical, since τούτῳ can only denote the unreal part of a pleasure or pain just spoken of. Unless we resort to emendation, we must suppose that Plato is, for the moment, thinking of the illusory part of the pleasure or pain as belonging not (as has been implied throughout this section) to the feeling itself, but to the external object, or situation, towards which the feeling is directed. Such a confusion is very apt to occur in Greek, in view of the ambiguity of such phrases as τὸ ἡδύ and τὸ λυπηρόν, and it may be observed that τὸ λυπηρόν was substituted for τὰς λύπας at B 4.

care about this sort of logical objection; he is concerned to analyse the different kinds of falsity or unreality that attach to anything that men call, rightly or wrongly, pleasure and pain. With the present section the reader should compare *Rep.* 583 B– 585 A, where the existence of a neutral state is established by an essentially similar argument; also *Timaeus* 64 C–65 B, where the same point is made as here about conscious and unconscious processes in connexion with pleasure.

The discussion in the *Republic* begins with an assertion, attributed to 'some wise person', that only the pleasure of the φρόνιμος is fully true, and later (584 C) it is declared that the majority of those pleasures that come through the body, and the greatest among them, are only reliefs from pain. The first of these statements is, however, afterwards modified in so far as purity is allowed to the pleasures of smell (as at *Phil.* 51 B), and to 'many others' which are not specified, but which should perhaps be identified with the pure aesthetic pleasures mentioned alongside those of smell in our dialogue. As to the second statement, it is to be noted that the λυπῶν ἀπαλλαγαί, that is to say the pleasures discussed in our present section, are the only sort of false or impure pleasures that are recognised in the *Republic*.

At 43 C–D it is remarked that we have discriminated three lives, the pleasant, the painful, and the neutral. This is the second triad of lives in our dialogue. The first (20 E ff.) was the life of pleasure, the life of intelligence, and the mixed life of pleasure and intelligence. Hence the life of pleasure is common to both triads, and the reason for there being two is probably to be found in contemporary anti-hedonist theories. In the first triad Hedonism is set against the doctrine, seemingly professed by some Socratics and perhaps by the historical Socrates himself, that φρόνησις is the good for man; this antithesis of ἡδονή and φρόνησις is mentioned at *Rep.* 505 B, and it is from it that the main ethical theory of our dialogue is developed. In the second triad Hedonism is confronted by the doctrine of the 'neutral' or 'middle' life (ὁ μέσος βίος, 43 E), in which Plato's successor Speusippus placed the human good, holding that both pleasure and pain are evils opposed to each other and to the good;[1] his name for the μέσος βίος (according to Clement of Alexandria, quoted in *R.P.* § 356) was ἀοχλησία.

Socrates has already spoken of a life devoid of both pleasure and pain, at 21 E and 33 B, and in both places he has associated it, and almost identified it, with the life of φρόνησις. Such a life is 'perhaps the most godlike of all lives' (33 B): but if it is θειότατος, it is not ἀνθρώπινος; no man would choose to live without some pleasure, as was agreed at 21 E.

Plato's concern in our present section is to establish the reality of the μέσος βίος, as against those who identified it either with pleasure

---

[1] See Burnet on Aristotle, *E.N.* 1153 B 1 and 1173 A 6.

or with pain; and so far he is in agreement with Speusippus, though whether Speusippus had already announced his theory we do not know: but for Plato it is of course not the μέσος βίος but the μεικτὸς βίος that constitutes the good for man. Nor does he suppose that there really is any μέσος βίος in the sense of a complete span of life, in which a man experiences neither pleasure nor pain: it is implied at 43 B–C that the μεγάλαι μεταβολαί are of frequent occurrence in every life.

Socrates   Protarchus

Soc. And next, if we take the road ahead of us,[1] we shall discern 42 C pleasures and pains in living beings that appear false and are false, even more so than this last kind.

Prot. What do you mean? What are they?

Soc. It has often been said,[2] I think, that when the natural state of an organism is impaired by processes of combination and separation, of filling and emptying, and by certain kinds of growth and decay, D the result is pain, distress, suffering—in fact everything that we denote by names like these.

Prot. Yes, that has often been said.

Soc. And when the organisms are being established in their natural state, we satisfied ourselves that that establishment is a pleasure.

Prot. And rightly so.

Soc. But suppose none of these processes is going on in our body.

Prot. When could that be so, Socrates?

Soc. There, Protarchus, you have put a question that is not to the E point.[3]

Prot. Why not?

---

[1] I follow Bury in printing commas after ὀψόμεθα and ἀπαντῶμεν.

[2] The reference here, unlike that in D 5–7 below (ἀπεδεξάμεθα παρ' ἡμῶν αὐτῶν), is not *directly* to the doctrine of 31 D ff., but to a fuller doctrine of which that is a part. In the former passage Plato had spoken of that sort of διάκρισις which is contrary to nature, and so breaks up the ἁρμονία of the organism, and that sort of πλήρωσις which is in accordance with nature, and so restores the ἁρμονία: and he had not spoken of σύγκρισις at all nor of αὔξη and φθίσις. Nevertheless the mention of παρὰ φύσιν πῆξις at 32 A implied that it is not only διάκρισις, but also σύγκρισις, that can be contrary to nature, and the following words πάλιν δ' εἰς ταὐτὸν ἀπιόντων καὶ διακρινομένων ἡ κατὰ φύσιν ὁδὸς ἡδονή implied, conversely, that it is not only σύγκρισις, but also διάκρισις, that can be according to nature. The full doctrine must be that all the processes, combination and separation, filling and emptying, growth and wastage, are sometimes κατὰ φύσιν, sometimes παρὰ φύσιν. In our present passage it is the occurrence of all these processes παρὰ φύσιν that is singled out for mention.

[3] Socrates means that, although it is never the case that none of these processes is going on, yet the fact that they are often, as will appear, unconscious justifies him in making his supposition.

Soc. Because you don't prevent me from repeating my own enquiry.

Prot. What enquiry?

Soc. What I shall say is, supposing, Protarchus, that nothing of the kind were to be going on, what inference should we have to draw?

Prot. You mean, if the body is not experiencing movement in either direction?

Soc. Yes.

Prot. Then one thing at all events is plain, Socrates; in such a case there can be no pleasure and no pain.

43 *Soc.* You are perfectly right. But I expect you are going to tell me that we are assured by the wise that one of these processes must always be going on in us, since all things are always flowing up and down.

Prot. Yes, they do assert that, and it is thought to carry some weight.

Soc. Naturally; they are weighty persons. But as a matter of fact I should like to dodge this argument that is advancing upon us. Here is my intended line of retreat, on which I hope you will accompany me.

Prot. Please explain the direction.

Soc. Let us reply to them 'so be it'; but here is a question for
B yourself: is a living being always conscious of everything that happens to it? Do we invariably notice that we are growing, and so on, or is that quite the reverse of the truth?

Prot. Surely it is absolutely the reverse: almost all such processes pass unnoticed by us.

Soc. Then we are not right in what was said just now, to the effect that changes up and down produce pains and pleasures.

Prot. Of course not.

C *Soc.* I will suggest a better formula, and one less open to attack.

Prot. Yes?

Soc. Great changes cause us pains and pleasures, but moderate and small ones cause no pain or pleasure whatsoever.

Prot. You are nearer the truth than you were, Socrates.

Soc. Then, if that be so, here we are back again at the life we mentioned a while ago.

Prot. What life?

Soc. The one we described as painless, and devoid of joys.

Prot. Very true.

Soc. In view of this, let us recognise three sorts of life, the pleasant,
D the painful, and that which is neither one nor the other. Or how do you see the matter?

Prot. I see it precisely as you put it: the lives are three in number.

Soc. Then to be without pain will not be the same as to feel pleasure?

Prot. Certainly not.

Soc. So when you hear someone say that the pleasantest of all things is to live one's whole life long without pain, what do you take his meaning to be?

Prot. He appears to me to mean that being without pain is pleasant.

Soc. Well now, let us take any three things you like; and, to give E them more attractive names, call the first gold, the second silver, and the third neither gold nor silver.

Prot. I accept that.

Soc. Now can we possibly identify the third with either of the others, with gold or silver?

Prot. No, of course not.

Soc. Similarly then, it cannot be right either to hold the inter-mediate life to be pleasant or painful, if it is a question of holding an opinion, or, to speak of it so, if it is a question of speaking; unless indeed we desert right reasoning.

Prot. It cannot.

Soc. Still, my friend, we do observe people saying and thinking so. 44

Prot. We do, certainly.

Soc. Do they then think that at such times as they are not feeling pain they are feeling pleasure?

Prot. They say so at all events.

Soc. Then they do think so; otherwise they would not say so, I imagine.

Prot. Maybe.

Soc. Nevertheless their opinion about their feeling of pleasure is false, if not being pained and feeling pleasure are really two different things.

Prot. And different they have certainly proved.

44 A–47 B   *Are any pleasures true? Examination of the extreme anti-hedonist position, beginning with mixed bodily pleasures*

We have found three distinct kinds of false pleasure, and it is beginning to look as if there were no true pleasures to be found. This is what certain thinkers, here described as the 'enemies of Philebus', 'dour persons' (δυσχερεῖς) and 'reputed experts in natural science' (δεινοὺς λεγομένους τὰ περὶ φύσιν), in fact believe. They deny the existence of our three states, recognising only two, pain and escape from pain. Though Socrates does not accept their view, he is sympathetic towards it: it is, he says, the outcome of a not ignoble nature; and if we follow it up, we shall very likely find it helpful. When we have finished with it, Socrates promises that he will describe what he regards as true pleasures (44 D).

The development of the anti-hedonist view which follows should probably be regarded as Plato's own.[1] The principle on which it proceeds is to examine pleasure in its intensest form, for this is likely to reveal its nature most truly. Now the intensest pleasures are those of the sick, whether in body or soul (45 E), and if we select some of these we shall find that they are mixed with pain: the mixture may be wholly in the body,[2] or wholly in the soul, or in both together. Taking the first kind to begin with, Socrates vividly illustrates first those cases where the pain, and secondly those where the pleasure predominates. The excessive enjoyment of these latter is the mark of the fool and the profligate.

It will be noticed that in this section Plato no longer speaks of *false* pleasures and pains but of *mixed*, or of a mixture of pleasure and pain. No real distinction seems intended between the two pairs, false-true, mixed-unmixed; for later on, when we come to the ingredients of the good life, we find that it is 'true' pleasures that are admitted (62 E), or 'true and pure pleasures' (ἡδονὰς ἀληθεῖς καὶ καθαράς, 63 E), where the adjectives are evidently both applied to the same kinds of pleasures.

The reason for the change of terminology in the present section, a change which persists all through the development of the anti-hedonist position (namely down to 51 A, where its defenders are recalled and taken leave of), is probably simply this, that when we are considering pleasure from the point of view of the 'three states' of 43 E the term 'false' is most conveniently reserved for the feelings which constitute the middle or neutral state, and which have been shown to be false pleasures and pains in the previous section. If Plato had continued to use the term 'false' for the types of pleasure now analysed, he would have obscured for the reader the extent to which he agreed with, and differed from, the anti-hedonists: which is just this, that though the so-called pleasures of the neutral state are for him, as 'for them, no pleasures at all, nevertheless there are real pleasures—pleasures that are not mere λυπῶν ἀποφυγαί—which however are not unmixed, but united with pain.

A second reason for the new terminology is perhaps that it prepares[3]

---

[1] With μεταδιώκωμεν δὴ τούτους at 44 D compare the treatment of Protagoras in the *Theaetetus*, prefaced by the words ἐπακολουθήσωμεν οὖν αὐτῷ at 152 B; also Ar. *Met*. 985 A 4 εἰ γάρ τις ἀκολουθοίη καὶ λαμβάνοι πρὸς τὴν διάνοιαν καὶ μὴ πρὸς ἃ ψελλίζεται λέγων Ἐμπεδοκλῆς κτλ.

[2] In the sense explained at p. 61 above.

[3] καθαρός is first used of pleasures at 52 C, if we accept Burnet's excision of καθαρὰς λυπῶν at 51 B.

the way for the use of καθαρός, with its associations of religious and moral purity. Now that he is beginning to study the *pathology* of pleasure and pain, their connexion with the sickness or disease of body or mind, Plato naturally tends to turn to moral and religious, rather than logical and intellectual categories. It is the badness of most pleasures, quite as much as their falsity, that should exclude them from the good life.

Who are the 'dour' or 'rigorous' (δυσχερεῖς) enemies of Philebus, with a 'great reputation for natural science' (δεινοὺς λεγομένους τὰ περὶ φύσιν, 44 B)? In view of the persistency with which their δυσχέρεια is emphasised (44 C6, D2, D8, E4), and of the combination of two characteristics, hostility to so-called pleasure, and scientific repute, there can be no doubt that Plato alludes to some definite person or persons; and since the *Philebus* is written with an eye to current controversy about pleasure, and cares little about anachronisms,[1] the allusion is almost certainly to some contemporaries. But to identify these seems impossible: the plain truth is that we know of none who 'deny the existence of pleasures altogether': not the Cynics, with whom Apelt confidently identifies the δυσχερεῖς; for even if there was a Cynic 'school' at this date, this was not their view:[2] not Democritus, for if we admit the authenticity of Frag. 4 (Diels-Kranz)—and there is almost nothing else to argue from—he held that 'the limit of what is and is not beneficial is τέρψις and ἀτερψίη' (which are seemingly synonyms for ἡδονή and λύπη, and are accordingly translated by Diels-Kranz 'Lust und Unlust'): not Speusippus, for a combination of Arist. *E.N.* 1153 B 1–7 with 1173 A 5–9 shows that he regarded pleasure and pain as both real, and both opposed to the neutral state, whereas the δυσχερεῖς admit not three states, but only two. The most likely, or I would rather say the least unlikely identification that has been suggested is that of Grote,[3] with whom Adam (Appendix IV to Book IX in his edition of the *Republic*) is in virtual agreement: the persons in question are 'probably Pythagorising friends' of Plato, 'who, adopting a ritual of extreme rigour, distinguished themselves by the violence of their antipathies towards τὰς ἡδονὰς τῶν ἀσχημόνων'. But it was quite possible to be an enemy of pleasure, or to deny the existence of pleasure, without being a Pythagorean or even Pythagorising: and it may be doubted whether δεινοὶ τὰ περὶ φύσιν is a very likely description of Pythagoreans. We must be content to leave the δυσχερεῖς unidentified. After all, it is quite probable that a view so extreme, and refuted so convincingly as this is in the present dialogue, would be short-lived and leave no record of its champions. It is noteworthy

[1] Even Prof. Taylor has no compunction in letting Socrates allude here to Speusippus, who cannot have reached years of discretion when Socrates died (*Comm. on Timaeus*, p. 456; *Plato*, p. 423).
[2] As Prof. Taylor reminds us, they held that ἡδονὰς τὰς μετὰ τοὺς πόνους διωκτέον, ἀλλ' οὐχὶ τὰς πρὸ τῶν πόνων (Stobaeus, *apud R.P.* § 280).
[3] *Plato*, II, p. 610.

that, amongst the many Hedonist and anti-hedonist views mentioned in *E.N.* vii and x, that which denies the existence of *any* pleasure is not found. It may be added that the δυσχερεῖς cannot be the σοφοί of *Rep.* 583 B (as Adam and others have supposed), for they held there was at least one true pleasure: οὐδὲ παναληθής ἐστιν ἡ τῶν ἄλλων ἡδονὴ πλὴν τῆς τοῦ φρονίμου οὐδὲ καθαρά.

Socrates   *Protarchus*

44A   *Soc.* Then are we to take the line that these things are three in
B number, as we said just now, or that they are only two, pain being an evil for mankind, and release from pain being called pleasant as in itself a good?

Prot. How can we put that question to ourselves, Socrates, at this stage? I don't understand.

Soc. The fact is, Protarchus, you don't understand what enemies Philebus here has.[1]

Prot. What enemies do you mean?

Soc. People with a great reputation for natural science, who maintain that pleasures do not exist at all.

Prot. O, how so?

Soc. What Philebus and his friends call pleasures are, according to
C them, never anything but escapes from pains.

Prot. And do you recommend that we should believe them, Socrates, or what do you think?

Soc. Not believe them, but avail ourselves of their gift of divination, which rests not on science but on the dourness, if I may call it so, of a nature far from ignoble: they are men who have come to hate pleasure[2] bitterly, to regard it as thoroughly unsound; its very
D attractiveness they regard, not as real pleasure, but as trickery. Well, you may avail yourself of their doctrine on this point, having regard at the same time to their other dour characteristics; and next you shall learn what pleasures I regard[3] as true, so that when we have examined the nature of pleasure from both points of view we may have a comparative basis for our decision.

Prot. Very good.

---

[1] Bury seems clearly right in printing this sentence as a statement, not a question.

[2] I agree with Souilhé (*Étude sur le terme* δύναμις, p. 120) that τὴν τῆς ἡδονῆς δύναμιν here is merely periphrastic.

[3] Reading γ' ἐμοί with Friedländer.

Soc. Then let us follow up the track of these allies of ours, and see where their dour footsteps lead us. I fancy that their basic position is stated something like this: if we want to see the true nature of any form, whatever it may be, for example that of hardness, should we E understand it best by fixing our attention on the hardest things there are or on those that have a minimum of hardness? Now, Protarchus, you must answer our dour friends just as you would answer me.

Prot. Quite so, and I tell them that our attention must be fixed on what has the maximum amount.

Soc. Then if the form or kind whose true nature we wanted to see were pleasure, we should have to fix our attention not on minimum pleasures but on such as are said to be the highest and intensest.   45

Prot. Everyone would agree with what you say now.

Soc. Now are not our obvious pleasures, which are in fact by common admission the greatest, the pleasures of the body?

Prot. Of course.

Soc. And are they, or do they become,[1] greater with those who are suffering from sickness or with healthy people? Now let us be careful not to take a false step by answering hastily. I dare say we shall be inclined to say, with healthy people.   B

Prot. Probably.

Soc. But tell me, are not the outstanding pleasures those which are preceded by the greatest desires?

Prot. That is true.

Soc. And isn't it the man suffering from a fever or some similar complaint who feels thirst and cold and all the common bodily troubles more than others, who is more than others acquainted with want, and who when the want comes to be satisfied[2] has greater pleasures? Shall we not admit that to be true?

Prot. Yes, it certainly seems true, now you put it so.

Soc. Well then, should we be plainly right if we said that anyone c wishing to see the greatest pleasures should direct his attention not to health, but to sickness? You must be careful not to take me as intending to ask you whether the extremely sick have *more* pleasures

---

[1] καὶ γίγνονται in A 7 is added as a hint that all Pleasure is Becoming, not Being—the doctrine announced at 53 C.

[2] ἀποπληρούμενοι is required at 45 B 9, not the genitive, which could only be governed by μείζους. Socrates is not saying that sick people have greater pleasures than those being replenished, but that sick people when they are replenished have greater pleasures than healthy people.

than the healthy: you must realise that it is the magnitude of pleasure that I am concerned with; I am asking where instances of the extreme in point of magnitude are to be found. We must, as we said, understand the true nature of pleasure, and what account they give who maintain that there is no such thing at all.

D   *Prot.* I follow your meaning pretty well.

Soc. I dare say, Protarchus, you will do just as well as my guide. Tell me this: in a profligate existence do you find greater pleasures—not *more* pleasures, mind you, but pleasures that stand out as extreme or in point of degree—than in a life of temperance? Give your mind to it, and tell me.

Prot. I understand your point, and I find a wide difference. The temperate man, surely, is regularly restrained by the proverbial warning

E   'Never too much', and heeds it; whereas the senseless profligate is mastered by his extreme pleasure, which ultimately drives him insane and makes him the talk of the town.

Soc. Right; then if that is so, clearly the greatest pleasures, and the greatest pains too, occur not when soul and body are good, but when they are bad.

Prot. Certainly.

Soc. And now we ought to select some of these and consider what characteristic made us call them the greatest.

46   *Prot.* Yes, we must.

Soc. Well, here is a type of malady, with pleasures whose characteristics I should like you to examine.

Prot. What type is it?

Soc. The offensive type, with its pleasures which are so thoroughly distasteful to the dour people we were speaking of.

Prot. What pleasures are they?

Soc. Relieving an itch, for example, by rubbing, and anything that calls for that sort of remedy. When we find ourselves experiencing that kind of thing, what, in heaven's name, are we to call it? Pleasure or pain?

Prot. Well that, Socrates, I really think might be described as a mixed experience.[1]

B   *Soc.* Of course I did not introduce the subject with any reference

---

[1] Reading πάθος for κακόν at A 13. συμμεικτὸν κακόν could only mean a composite evil, and there is no reason why Protarchus should regard the pleasant factor here as evil.

to Philebus; but without a look at these pleasures and others associated with them I hardly think we shall be able to settle the question before us.

Prot. Then we must proceed to attack the kindred pleasures.

Soc. You mean those that share that characteristic of mixture?

Prot. Exactly.

Soc. Well, some of the mixtures concern the body and are found in the body alone, while others are found in the soul and belong to the c soul alone; and thirdly we shall discover cases of pains being mixed with pleasures that involve both soul and body, where the total experience is sometimes called pleasure, sometimes pain.

Prot. What do you mean?

Soc. When the natural state of an organism is being established or impaired, it may be subject to two opposite experiences at once: it may be warmed while shivering, or again cooled while burning: it is seeking, I imagine, to attain one thing and get rid of the other; and the 'bitter-sweet' mixture, if I may use the current phrase, when it is hard to get rid of the thing, causes an uneasiness which develops into fierce excitement. D

Prot. What you are now saying is very true.

Soc. Now in mixtures like these are not the pains and pleasures sometimes equal, while sometimes one or the other predominates?

Prot. Of course.

Soc. In the class in which the pains predominate over the pleasures you must count those pleasures of itching that we were speaking of, and of tickling: when the irritation or inflammation is internal, and by rubbing and scratching you fail to reach it and merely tear the E surface skin, then, by bringing the parts affected near a fire and seeking to reverse your condition by means of the heat it gives out, you procure at one moment immense pleasure, at another a contrast between interior and exterior, a combination of pains with pleasures, the balance tilting now this way now that; this being due to the forcible tearing apart of what was compact or the compressing of what was diffused.[1] 47

Prot. Very true.

Soc. On the other hand when anything of this kind is happening and

---

[1] In this difficult paragraph I have adopted Burnet's πυρίαις in E 2, but removed his dashes in D 8 and 9. I take εἰς τοὐναντίον πυρίαις μεταβάλλοντες to mean 'trying to reverse the condition of interior heat and exterior coolness by applications of heat to the exterior'. The final words καὶ ὁμοῦ λύπας ἡδοναῖς παρατιθέναι I have omitted, for they seem to yield no sense and must, I think, be a foolish gloss on τὰ διακεκριμένα συγχεῖν. The sentence is complete without them, and the mixture of pains and pleasures has already been expressed in E 3–4.

pleasure preponderates in the mixture, although the slight element of pain causes a tickling and a mild uneasiness, yet the inflowing stream of pleasure, which is much stronger, excites you and sometimes makes you jump for joy: it produces all manner of varieties in your complexion, in your attitude, in the very breath you draw, and drives you clean out of your wits, shouting aloud like a lunatic.

B   *Prot.* Yes indeed.

Soc. And what's more, my friend, it makes people say of themselves, and makes others say of them, that they are almost dying of delight in these pleasures: and I would add that the more of a fool and profligate a man is, the more wholeheartedly is he sure to pursue them, calling them the greatest pleasures and accounting such as have the greatest amount thereof in their lives the happiest of beings.

47 B–50 E   *Mixed pleasures of Body and Soul, and of Soul alone. Examination of malice (φθόνος), especially as felt by the spectator of comedy*

Besides (1) the mixed pleasures and pains of bodily origin first examined, there are (2) those of body and soul together, and (3) those of soul alone. The second sort are here dismissed briefly, for we have noticed them already: they are found when pleasurable anticipation coincides with the pain of organic depletion (36 B). But the third sort are peculiarly interesting to Plato, who singles out for special treatment the feeling or emotion of malice (φθόνος). His discussion is however confined for the most part to one particular type of malice, namely that felt at the misfortunes of a comic character on the stage; he seems to feel that in taking this he is taking a difficult, yet illuminating type (48 B), and that if we can succeed in understanding it we shall readily understand not only other kinds of malice, but the other 'mixed pleasures of soul' as well.[1]

---

[1] I have adopted the rendering 'malice' for φθόνος from Prof. Taylor; Apelt uses sometimes 'Neid', sometimes 'Missgunst'; Bury has 'envy' and C. Ritter (*Platon*, II, p. 439) 'Schadenfreude'. The word is defined by Aristotle (*Topics*, 109 B 36) as λύπη ἐπὶ φαινομένῃ εὐπραγίᾳ τῶν ἐπιεικῶν τινός: cf. *Rhet.* 1387 B 21. This restriction of the objects of the emotion to good men corresponds to Plato's restriction of them at 49 D to φίλοι as opposed to ἐχθροί; and the reason for it doubtless is that φθόνος was commonly felt to be wrong or culpable (cf. *E.N.* 1107 A 9 ἔνια γὰρ εὐθὺς ὠνόμασται συνειλημμένα μετὰ τῆς φαυλότητος, οἷον ἐπιχαιρεκακία ἀναισχυντία φθόνος). Now the envy we feel at a good man's good fortune is commonly linked with a desire for his hurt; hence, as applied to real life, φθόνος may well be rendered as 'malicious envy'. But what we feel towards the comic character, what Plato calls παιδικὸς φθόνος (49 A), the φθόνος involved in an entertaining spectacle, is an emotion in which both the envy and the malice are only half-real: we half envy the pretentious character (e.g. the *miles gloriosus*) before his pretentions are exposed, because we half believe them; we feel quasi-malicious,

We start with the premiss that malice, though painful, includes pleasure at the troubles or defects[1] of our neighbours. But since this pleasure is comic, that is to say aroused by what is laughable or ridiculous, we must discover what kinds of defect are ridiculous. By a series of logical divisions of τὸ κακόν or πονηρία (badness) we arrive at the notion of a man's false conceit of wisdom or cleverness; but this is only ridiculous when the man is weak, in the sense that he lacks the power to retaliate on those who disagree with him or oppose him. Malice, then, is felt towards the harmless braggart of the stage. But now a fresh point arises. Malice is commonly regarded as a wrongful emotion, and since there is nothing wrongful in rejoicing at the troubles of our enemies, it follows that the victim of our malice must be a friend. In saying this Plato seems to be passing from the stage to real life. Comic stage characters are neither our friends nor our enemies;[2] this is true at least of the fourth-century stage: a Cleon or a Euripides might be, but that is another matter, and Plato is not thinking of the Old Comedy. Nor is the comic emotion felt by anybody to be wrongful; what is wrongful, yet at the same time fraught with amusement, is the emotion of φθόνος aroused by the sight of a vainglorious 'friend' (by which no more is meant than one who is not an enemy) being 'deflated' or 'debunked'. And this is a mixed emotion, since the very condition of our pleasure is the pain caused by another's seeming superiority to ourselves.

This extension of view, from the φθόνος of the comic spectator to that of real life, lends an additional importance to Plato's discussion of this emotion; and unless we do so interpret it, we can hardly comprehend his allusion to the 'whole tragi-comedy of life' at 50 B.

| *Protarchus* | *Socrates* |

Prot. Everything, Socrates, that most people agree in thinking, is 47 B covered by your exposition.

Soc. Yes, Protarchus, as far as concerns those pleasures in which it c is merely the body's superficial and internal parts that are interconnected in mutual affections. But there are cases in which the soul's contribution

we want him to be made to look ridiculous, 'taken down', but our malice is weakened by our knowledge that in fact he is going to be. This semi-reality of painful emotion is of the essence of Comedy, or at least of the kind of Comedy known to fourth-century Athens. The φθόνος is παιδικός: it is 'all a joke', or nearly all.

[1] ἐπὶ κακοῖς τοῖς τῶν πέλας, 48 B. κακά here is not so narrow as 'misfortunes': it means anything not ἀγαθόν or καλόν, and would include poverty or ugliness or low birth. Yet in the sequel it is narrowly restricted, doubtless in conformity with the current restrictions of fourth-century Comedy.

[2] They may of course be likable, 'sympathetic', or the reverse; and this is how Prof. Taylor interprets φίλοι and ἐχθροί here. But I doubt whether the words admit of this attenuated meaning.

is opposed to that of the body, whether it be pain as against the body's pleasure or pleasure as against the body's pain, so that the two[1] unite to form a single compound. These we discussed previously, showing that at such times as we are emptied we desire replenishment, and that we delight in the expectation of replenishment but are distressed by the process of emptying; but there is one thing that we did not declare

D then but assert now, namely that in all these innumerable instances in which soul is at variance with body, we find a single type of the mixture of pain and pleasure.

Prot. I am inclined to think you are quite right.

Soc. And now we have still left one more mixture of pain and pleasure.

Prot. Which is that?

Soc. That mingling which, as we mentioned,[2] the soul alone takes to itself.

Prot. In what sense do we maintain that?[3]

E *Soc.* Anger, fear, longing, lamenting, love, emulation, malice and so forth—don't you class these as pains of the soul itself?

Prot. I do.

Soc. And shall we not find them replete with immense pleasures? Or need we remind ourselves of that feature of passion and anger[4]— of the lines:

'Wrath that spurs on the wisest mind to rage,
Sweeter by far than stream of flowing honey',

48 or of the pleasures mixed up with the pains in lamentation and longing?

Prot. No: what you say is precisely what must happen.

Soc. Then again do you remember how spectators of a tragedy sometimes feel pleasure and weep at once?

Prot. Yes indeed.

Soc. And if you take the state of our minds when we see a comedy, do you realise that here again we have a mixture of pain and pleasure?

Prot. I don't quite take your meaning.

B *Soc.* No, Protarchus, for it is by no means easy to understand that we are regularly affected in this way on such an occasion.

---

[1] ἀμφότερα in c 5 means the contributions of soul and body.
[2] This has not, in fact, been mentioned. It may be a slip, cf. 34 E: if not, Bury's φαμέν for ἔφαμεν should be accepted in D 9.
[3] αὖ (Ast) seems a necessary correction for αὐτό in D 10.
[4] I retain Burnet's text here, but remove his brackets.

Prot. It certainly does not seem easy to me.

Soc. Still, the obscurity of the matter ought to make us all the more eager to grasp it; we may make it easier for people to realise the mixture of pain and pleasure in other cases.

Prot. Pray go on.

Soc. We mentioned malice just now: would you call that a pain of the soul, or what?

Prot. Yes.

Soc. Nevertheless one will find the malicious man pleased at his neighbours' ills.

Prot. Undoubtedly.   c

Soc. Now ignorance, or the condition we call stupidity, is an ill thing.[1]

Prot. Well?

Soc. That being so, observe the nature of the ridiculous.

Prot. Be kind enough to tell me.

Soc. Taking it generally it is a certain kind of badness, and it gets its name from a certain state of mind. I may add that it is that species of the genus 'badness' which is differentiated by the opposite of the inscription at Delphi.[2]

Prot. You mean 'Know thyself', Socrates?

Soc. I do. Plainly the opposite of that would be for the inscription D to read 'By no means know thyself'.

Prot. Of course.

Soc. Now, Protarchus, that is what you must split up into three parts: see if you can.

Prot. How do you mean? I am quite sure I can't.

Soc. Do you then mean that I must make this division, here and now?

Prot. That is what I mean, and indeed I beg you to do so.

Soc. If anyone does not know himself, must it not be in one of three ways?

Prot. How so?

Soc. First, in respect of wealth; he may think himself richer than E his property makes him.

---

[1] There is a problem of translation here which I cannot solve. Socrates uses the same word, κακόν, for what we should naturally call a trouble (or misfortune) and a vice (or moral defect). There is no real equivocation; yet English needs different words, and in falling back on 'ill' I am conscious of failure.

[2] The language here is intended to be whimsically obscure.

Prot. Plenty of people are affected that way, certainly.

Soc. But there are even more who think themselves taller and more handsome and physically finer in general than they really and truly are.

Prot. Quite so.

Soc. But far the greatest number are mistaken as regards the third class of things, namely possessions of the soul: they think themselves superior in virtue, when they are not.

Prot. Yes indeed.

49 *Soc.* And is it not the virtue of wisdom that the mass of men insist on claiming, interminably disputing, and lying about how wise they are?

Prot. Of course.

Soc. And certainly we should be justified in calling all such behaviour as this evil.

Prot. Undoubtedly.

Soc. Well now, Protarchus, it is this that we must once more divide, by bisection, if we mean to see that curious mixture of pleasure and pain that lies in the malice that goes with entertainment. How then, you B will ask, do we make our bisection? All persons who are foolish enough to hold this false opinion about themselves fall, I think, like mankind in general, into two classes, those who are strong and powerful and those who are the reverse.

Prot. Indubitably.

Soc. Then make that your principle of division. Those whose delusion is accompanied by weakness, who are unable to retaliate when laughed at, you will be right in describing by the epithet 'ridiculous'; c to those that have the ability and strength to retaliate you will most appropriately accord the epithets 'formidable' and 'hateful'. For ignorance in the strong is hateful and ugly: it is fraught with mischief to all around, and so are its copies on the stage; but weak ignorance ranks as the ridiculous, which in fact it is.

Prot. You are perfectly right. All the same, I am not yet clear about the mixture of pleasures and pains here.

Soc. Well, take first the nature of malice.

Prot. Pray continue.

D *Soc.* Both pain and pleasure can be wrongful, I imagine?

Prot. Unquestionably.

Soc. And to delight in our enemies' misfortunes is neither wrongful nor malicious?

Prot. Of course not.

Soc. Whereas to feel delight, as we sometimes do, instead of pain, when we see friends in misfortune, is wrongful, is it not?

Prot. Of course.

Soc. Now we said that ignorance is always an evil?

Prot. That is so.

Soc. Then if we find in our friends that imaginary wisdom and imaginary beauty, and the other delusions which we enumerated in our E threefold classification just now, delusions that are ridiculous in the weak and hateful in the strong—if we find this disposition in its harmless form in our friends, shall we adhere, or shall we not, to my statement of a moment ago, namely that it is ridiculous?

Prot. Certainly we shall.

Soc. And do we not agree that, being ignorance, it is evil?

Prot. Undoubtedly.

Soc. And when we laugh at it, are we pleased or pained?

Prot. Plainly we are pleased. 50

Soc. And did we not say that it is malice that makes us feel pleasure in our friends' misfortunes?

Prot. It must be.

Soc. The upshot of our argument then is that when we laugh at what is ridiculous in our friends, we are mixing pleasure this time with malice, mixing, that is, our pleasure with pain; for we have been for some time agreed that malice is a pain in the soul, and that laughter is a pleasure, and both occur simultaneously on the occasions in question.

Prot. True.

Soc. Hence our argument now makes it plain that in laments and B tragedies and comedies—and not only in those of the stage but in the whole tragi-comedy of life—as well as on countless other occasions, pains are mixed with pleasures.

Prot. The most determined of opponents could not but agree with what you say, Socrates.

Soc. Moreover we made a list including anger, longing, lamentation, fear, love, malice and so on, in all of which we said that we should find c our oft-repeated mixture; did we not?

Prot. Yes.

Soc. Then do we realize that what we have just discussed was all concerned with lamentation, malice and anger?

Prot. I am sure we do.

Soc. That being so, is there still much left to discuss?

Prot. Yes indeed.

Soc. Now what exactly do you suppose was my purpose in pointing out the mixture in comedy? Was it not to give you a ground for
D believing that it would be easy enough to demonstrate the same mingling in the case of fear, love, and the rest? I hoped that, having grasped the first example, you would relieve me of the necessity of entering upon a long argument about the others, and would grasp the general principle, that whether the body be affected apart from the soul, or the soul apart from the body, or both of them together, we constantly come upon the mixture of pleasure with pain. So tell me now, are you going to relieve me or will you keep me up till midnight? I fancy I shall secure your consent to release me if I just add this, that
E I shall be willing to go into the whole question with you to-morrow, but for the present I want to address myself to the matters which are still outstanding if we are to settle the problem set us by Philebus.

50 E–52 B   *Types of true pleasures*

We have now finished with the 'dour thinkers', and Socrates proceeds to fulfil his promise (44 D) of enumerating the types of true pleasures. Their common characteristic is the absence of pain, whether simultaneous, antecedent or subsequent; and although Plato does not make the point very clearly, they appear to fall into two classes according as they are or are not accompanied by the apprehension of beauty. The former class is a 'sublime kind of pleasure' (θεῖον γένος ἡδονῶν, 51 E): it consists of the pleasures of seeing certain simple shapes—straight lines, curves, planes and solids—and simple colours, and of hearing single musical notes. What is stressed in regard to these objects (51 C6, D7) is that they are beautiful, and moreover intrinsically, not relatively beautiful: that is to say, their beauty does not depend on contrast with something less beautiful, or positively ugly, but belongs to them *per se*.

To the second class belong, in the first place, pleasures of smell; in these there is no admixture of necessary pains, and this justifies us in reckoning them as co-ordinate with those just mentioned; yet they are of less value, a less 'sublime' kind. Why is this? Doubtless just because they do not involve the apprehension of beauty: their objects (not of course the odorous *things*, but the actual odours) do not in any way exemplify unity in variety, or the relation of symmetry in a whole of parts.[1]

At their first mention, Socrates restricts them to '*most* of the pleasures of smell' (51 B4). This is probably because some are pleasant only by way of contrast with antecedent unpleasant odours, apart from which they would be faint or even non-existent.

In the *Phaedrus* (250 D) Plato had confined the perception of beauty to the sense of sight, 'the keenest of the senses'; here he extends it to hearing, but with both senses he limits it to the perception of objects of a very simple nature, pure colours, regular shapes, and single musical notes; living creatures and pictures are explicitly ruled out, as also by implication are all the products of the fine arts, as well as the beauties of Nature. All these must be reckoned as not amongst the καλὰ καθ' αὐτά, but as πρός τι καλά. They are, that is to say, relatively beautiful in the sense that they come at some point on a scale of greater and less aesthetic satisfaction. But the καλὰ καθ' αὐτά are such that no greater sensible beauty could be conceived: they are, it seems, perfect particulars of the Idea of Beauty, its fully adequate expression to sense.[1]

It is in this passage that Plato seems to come nearest to formulating what Bosanquet[2] calls 'the one true aesthetic principle recognised by Hellenic antiquity in general...the principle that beauty consists in the imaginative or sensuous expression of unity in variety'. Beauty, as here conceived, is a differentiated unity, but a unity with the very minimum of differentiation: the pure colour is a whole of parts simply inasmuch as it is a unity extended in space, the pure note is a whole of parts inasmuch as it is a unity extended in time; the same principle applies to straight lines and to elementary geometrical forms which (to quote Bosanquet again) 'are among the purest examples of unity in the form of simple regular or symmetrical shape'.

This is not the place for a discussion of Plato's general attitude to Art, for which the reader may be referred to the penetrating treatment in Bosanquet's third and fourth chapters. The exclusion in our present passage of ζῷα and ζωγραφήματα from the list of intrinsically beautiful things, with all that that exclusion implies, is, I think, at bottom due to what the English critic calls the 'metaphysical principle' adopted by Plato, to the detriment of the full application of a genuine aesthetic principle: Art *imitates* 'commonplace reality', and is therefore an imperfect and inferior reduplication thereof rather than a symbolic expression of spiritual reality. The limited range of the καλὰ καθ' αὐτά here is a direct consequence of this attitude to Art.

The last kind of true pleasures are those of learning. These are indeed preceded by a want, and may, if we forget, be followed by a want; but the want is declared to be painless. Similarly in *Rep.* 585 B Plato speaks of a κενότης in this connexion, not (as Prof. Taylor rightly stresses[3]) of a κένωσις; it is not the being empty before we are filled,

---

[1] That Beauty holds a special place amongst the Ideas, in that it can be revealed to sense with a clearness that none other can, Plato has said in the *Phaedrus* (250 B–D). But there he looked for that revelation in a very different quarter. He approaches Beauty now not from the standpoint of erotic mysticism, but from that of aesthetic analysis. To seek to 'harmonise' these approaches is futile, for Plato's thought resists forcing into a single mould.

[2] *History of Aesthetic*, p. 30.

[3] *Commentary on Plato's Timaeus*, p. 451.

but the conscious process of becoming empty, that involves pain. But in saying that this kind of pleasure is enjoyed only by very few persons (52 B) Plato implies that he is using μαθήματα in a very restricted sense, the acquisition namely of truth in science, not the commonplace learning of daily experience. Whether such pleasure is for Plato more valuable than the pure pleasure in beauty he does not·tell us; but if it is, then his position is identical with that of Aristotle, who finds the highest pleasure in θεωρητικὴ ἐπιστήμη, the contemplation of attained truth in First Philosophy (Theology), Physics and Mathematics.

Protarchus   Socrates

50E   *Prot.* Very good, Socrates; deal with the outstanding points as you fancy.

Soc. Well, after the mixed pleasures we shall naturally go on in turn—indeed we can hardly avoid it—to the unmixed.

51   *Prot.* Excellent.

Soc. Then I will start afresh and try to indicate, to you and to myself, which they are. With those who maintain that all pleasures are a cessation of pains I am not altogether inclined to agree, but, as I said, I avail myself of their evidence that some pleasures are apparent and quite unreal, while others present themselves to us as being great and numerous, but are in fact jumbled up with pains and processes of relief from such severe suffering as besets both body and soul.

B   *Prot.* But which, Socrates, should we be justified in regarding as true?

Soc. Those that attach to colours that we call beautiful, to figures, to most odours, to sounds, and to all experiences in which the want is imperceptible and painless, but its fulfilment is perceptible and pleasant.

Prot. In what sense, Socrates, does what you say hold good of these?

Soc. Well, what I mean is not quite obvious immediately; however,
c I must try to explain it. The beauty of figures which I am now trying to indicate is not what most people would understand as such, not the beauty of a living creature or a picture; what I mean, what the argument points to,[1] is something straight, or round, and the surfaces and solids which a lathe, or a carpenter's rule and square, produces from the straight and the round. I wonder if you understand. Things like that, I maintain, are beautiful not, like most things, in a relative sense; they are always beautiful in their very nature, and they carry pleasures

---

[1] The argument (ὁ λόγος) is, as often, personified, and εὐθύ τι καὶ περιφερὲς... γωνίαις is, as we should say, within inverted commas.

50307

peculiar to themselves which are quite unlike the pleasures of scratching. D
And there are colours too which have this characteristic. Do we grasp
this? What do you say?

Prot. I am trying to do so, Socrates. Perhaps you too would try
to put it still more plainly.

Soc. Very well:[1] audible sounds which are smooth and clear, and
deliver a single series of pure notes, are beautiful not relatively to
something else, but in themselves, and they are attended by pleasures
implicit in themselves.

Prot. Yes, certainly that is so.

Soc. Odours provide pleasures of a less sublime type; but the fact E
that no necessary pains are mixed with them, as well as the general
character and source of the experience, induces me to class them as
cognate with those just mentioned. Here then, if you follow me, are
two of the types of pleasure we are now concerned with.

Prot. I follow you.

Soc. Now let us proceed to add to them the pleasures of learning,
if we do in fact think that they involve no hunger, that no initial 52
distress is felt owing to a hunger for learning.

Prot. I share that view.

Soc. But suppose one who has been filled with learning loses it
afterwards by forgetting it, do you find that such loss involves distress?

Prot. No, at least not to a man's natural self,[2] but by way of his
reflexion upon what has happened, when he feels pain because of the
usefulness of what he has lost. B

Soc. But you know, my dear fellow, we are concerned at present
only with the actual experiences of the natural self, apart from any
reflexions about them.

Prot. Then you are right in saying that in cases of forgetting what
we have learnt we feel no pain.

Soc. So we must assert that these pleasures of learning are unmixed
with pains, and that they belong not to the general run of men but
only to the very few.

Prot. Certainly.

[1] To Protarchus's request for explanation Socrates replies by giving additional
instances of true or pure pleasures, viz. those of sound, smell and learning. Plato
perhaps feels that the notion of truth is easier to grasp in these latter than in those
of shape and colour.

[2] It is difficult to render φύσει and φύσεως in A 8 and B 3. Plato seems to mean
that the pain at loss of knowledge is not something really belonging to the self,
but quasi-external, felt by an outside 'observer', as it were.

52 C–53 C   *Purity, not magnitude or intensity, is the mark of truth*

The pleasures just discussed have been described as unmixed (ἀμείκτους, 50 E) and also as true (ἀληθεῖς, 51 B). It is however somewhat puzzling, at first sight, that Plato should now raise the question whether purity, as applied to pleasure, is synonymous or co-extensive with truth. The explanation is probably to be found in his wish to establish a universal connexion between the two terms. He has, no doubt, used the two antithetical pairs, false-true, mixed-unmixed, more or less indifferently in reference to the actual types of pleasure which have come before us; sometimes one pair has been found more appropriate, sometimes the other; but, as we have remarked, no real difference has been intended. Yet such a procedure does not suffice to show that pure pleasures must always be true ones and *vice versa*; that is what he does now attempt to show, by generalising the application of the four terms through the illustration of 'whiteness'.

But that is not all: not less important than showing that purity is co-extensive with truth is to show that intensity or bulk is not. It might have been supposed, when we agreed that the φύσις of pleasure was to be discovered by looking at its intensest forms, that these forms were the truest pleasures. And indeed in one sense of 'true' perhaps they are; but not in the sense in which Plato uses the term. For him it denotes, primarily, correspondence with the notion of a thing—or, to put it in the terminology of his own metaphysic, participation in the Idea of a thing; hence the more a thing is mixed with its opposite, the less it corresponds with its notion, the less true it is. Now there is this paradox about pleasure, that the more intense, the greater in quantity it becomes, the more certainly, as we have seen, does it involve the admixture of its opposite, pain. From this it follows not merely, negatively, that bulk or intensity is not the criterion of truth in pleasure, but, positively, that measure or moderation is an essential attribute of true pleasure.

Ostensibly this is inconsistent with the earlier inclusion of all pleasure in the γένος τοῦ ἀπείρου, for the ἄπειρον is just that which lacks all quantitative determination. But we should be chary of accusing Plato of gross self-contradiction, more especially as we shall find Protarchus again declaring, with Socrates's emphatic approval, near the end of the dialogue, that 'there is nothing in the world more unmeasured (ἀμετρώτερον) than pleasure' (65 D).

The fact is that, for pleasure to be true, pure, measured, there must be added to its own nature something external to it; this is the converse of the paradox already mentioned. Two earlier passages have suggested this: 28 A, 'we must look for something other than the character of being unlimited to explain how an element of good attaches to pleasures', and 31 A, 'pleasure is itself unlimited, and belongs to the kind that does not and never will contain *within itself and derived from itself* (ἐν αὐτῷ ἀφ' ἑαυτοῦ) either beginning, or middle, or end'.

Pleasure is for Plato a feeling which, in its own nature, is not positively bad but is bad in the negative sense that it lacks the right determination without which nothing is good, the quality which a thing has when πέρας has been 'mixed' with it. Left to itself, pleasure tends to destroy itself, to become untrue to itself: in that sense its φύσις is seen in the σφοδραὶ ἡδοναί; the only true pleasures occur when it is not left to itself, but submits to the addition of a limit, which is both a determinant and a check.

That is the doctrine implied at 52 c. It is not, however, fully worked out. We should like to be told, but we never are, in what precise sense the various kinds of pure pleasure possess measure or limit, and how human intelligence functions in imposing such measure. That these pleasures do not *in fact* tend to run to excess as the ordinary sensual pleasures do is plain enough. Plato, however, seems content to leave this as a fact of experience, and instead of giving a positive account of the ἐμμετρία of the pure pleasures he leaves us with a merely negative idea of it as the absence of ἀμετρία. This is, I think, a serious gap in Plato's psychology, but it does not invalidate his ethical conclusions.

It may be objected that, although pleasure in the abstract belongs to the ἄπειρον γένος, any actual pleasure must be a μεικτόν of πέρας and ἄπειρον; it is the same as with Plato's own illustration of temperature: temperature in the abstract is an ἄπειρον, a τὸ μᾶλλόν τε καὶ ἧττον δεχόμενον, but any actual temperature is of a definite, determined degree. How then can Socrates say, as he does at 52 c, that intense pleasures belong to the ἄπειρον γένος (or, if γενεᾶς be read in 52 D 1, to the γενεὰ τοῦ ἀπείρου)?

Our answer should probably be that Plato's conception of τὸ ἄπειρον suffers from a certain inconsistency[1] as the result of his restriction of the class of μεικτά to good compounds (see p. 38 above). That restriction leads him to think of the emotional condition called σφοδρα ἡδονή not only as ἄμετρον—devoid of due measure or moderation—but also as ἄπειρον. It is not of course ἄπειρον in the sense of lacking *all* determination, for its very σφοδρότης is quantitative determination; but it is ἄπειρον in the sense that it is characterised by the possibility of indefinite advance beyond the point of ἐμμετρία. Violence of emotion is just this indefinite advance, this utter absence of check, which Philebus had acclaimed as the characteristic of pleasure at 27 E: οὐ γὰρ ἂν ἡδονὴ πανάγαθον ἦν, εἰ μὴ ἄπειρον ἐτύγχανε πεφυκὸς καὶ πλήθει καὶ τῷ μᾶλλον. To express this in the language used to describe μεικτά at 25 E–26 A, the soul of the ἀκόλαστος (or σφόδρα ἡδόμενος) is one in which there is no ὀρθὴ κοινωνία of Limit and Unlimited, and where in consequence it is not the case that τὸ πολὺ λίαν καὶ ἄπειρον has been removed and τὸ ἔμμετρον achieved.

[1] Here I follow Ritter (*Platon*, II, p. 171) in essentials, though perhaps he goes too far in speaking of a 'verwirrender Doppelsinn' of the term ἄπειρον.

Socrates   *Protarchus*

52 c   *Soc.* Well, we have reached the point of drawing a satisfactory line between pure pleasures and those that may with fair justification be called impure: and now let us add to our statement that those pleasures that are intense are marked by immoderateness, those that are not by moderation. Pleasures that can go to great lengths or to an intense degree, whether they actually do so often or seldom, let us class as belonging to that 'unlimited' kind of which we spoke, which pene-

D trates body and soul alike in greater or in less degree: but the other sort let us class amongst things moderate.[1]

Prot. You are quite right, Socrates.

Soc. And now there is yet another feature of them which we must look into.

Prot. What is that?

Soc. What are we to reckon as making for truth? That which is pure, perfectly clear and sufficient, or that which is extreme, vast and huge?[2]

Prot. What is the object of your question, Socrates?

Soc. My object, Protarchus, is to do all I can to determine whether some sorts of pleasure, and some sorts of knowledge also, are pure and

E others not pure: for if, in deciding about them, we can get each in its pure form, that will facilitate the decision which you and I and all of us here have to make.

Prot. Quite right.

Soc. Well then, I will suggest a general method for the consideration of anything we call pure: namely, that we should begin by examining one selected example.

53   *Prot.* And what are we to select?

Soc. First and foremost, if you like, let us contemplate whiteness.

Prot. By all means.

Soc. How shall we get a pure white? What will it be? The greatest possible quantity or bulk of it, or the white with the least possible admixture, with no portion of any other colour in its composition?

Prot. Plainly it will be the most perfectly clear colour.

---

[1] I have translated Burnet's text: but the sentence c 4–D 1 is corrupt, and even the general sense uncertain. Perhaps γενεᾶς should be read for γένους in D 1: cf. note on 30 E.

[2] In D 8 I accept Jackson's transposition of καὶ τὸ ἱκανόν, which gives two sets of three adjectives. ἱκανόν should not be altered to ἰταμόν (Burnet).

Soc. You are right. Then shall we not reckon that, Protarchus, as the truest of all white things, and the fairest too, rather than a great B quantity or bulk of the colour?

Prot. Quite right.

Soc. Then we shall be absolutely right in saying that a small quantity of pure white is not only whiter, but also fairer and truer, than a large quantity of mixed white.

Prot. Yes, perfectly.

Soc. What then? I imagine we shall not need numerous examples of the same sort to make a pronouncement about pleasure, but are now in a position to realise that any and every sort of pleasure that is pure of pain will be pleasanter, truer, and fairer than one that is not, what- c ever be their comparative bulk or quantity.

Prot. Unquestionably so: the example before us is sufficient.

53 C–55 A   *Pleasure as process: the contrast of means and end*

We have discriminated the pure and true pleasures from the mixed (impure) and false; and we have shown a universal connexion between truth (in the sense in which the term is applicable to pleasures and pains) and purity (unmixedness). It might now seem natural to proceed forthwith to a classification of forms of knowledge, which, as Socrates has admitted (14 B), require to be discriminated no less than the forms of pleasure. But Plato does not begin this until 55 C. The intervening pages contain an argument directed against the original thesis of Philebus, that pleasure is the good—a thesis which finds its clearest expression at 60 A, where he is said to maintain that the two terms, good and pleasant, are identical in meaning.

The section begins abruptly, and has no obvious connexion with what has immediately preceded. Moreover it seems puzzling that Plato should revert to a point of view which, by treating pleasure as a simple unity, appears to ignore the classification of its types. We should, I suggest, regard the section not as an integral part of the dialogue, but as a semi-independent discussion of a 'dialectical' character in the Aristotelian sense, one namely which proceeds from a premiss not known to be true, but having some measure of probability. A modern author would have relegated it to an appendix.

The chief reason for so taking it, apart from the fact that it treats pleasure as an undifferentiated unity, is the occurrence of the words ἡδονή γε εἴπερ γένεσίς ἐστιν twice within half-a-dozen lines at 54 C–D. This, I believe, is intended to show that the whole argument is provisional or tentative, that Plato does not endorse (though he does not reject) the premiss with which it starts; but he is grateful to its authors

(53 C7, 54 D6), because it leads to a conclusion with which he agrees, namely that pleasure cannot, as Philebus thinks, be the good for man. Socrates begins by recording a doctrine put forward by certain 'subtle' persons (κομψοί τινες),[1] that pleasure is always a 'becoming' or process (γένεσις), and that there is no being (οὐσία) of pleasure whatsoever. It seems likely that here again,[2] as in the case of the δυσχερεῖς, we have a reference to actual contemporary thinkers; the twice-expressed obligation (οἷς δεῖ χάριν ἔχειν) would be pointless save as a sincere acknowledgment. If they are to be identified at all, Speusippus and his followers alone will fill the bill; but this identification rests not so much on the fact that we have good reason to believe that Speusippus defined pleasure as γένεσις εἰς φύσιν αἰσθητή[3] as on the coincidence of the general argument in which Socrates here expands and develops the thesis with one attributed by Aristotle to certain radical anti-hedonists. To this we must return later.

Socrates's argument is not necessarily that of the κομψοί themselves; it may well be Plato's own development, though the introductory formula διαπερανοῦμαί σοι τοῦτ' αὐτὸ ἐπανερωτῶν is not decisive on this point. In substance he argues as follows: the antithesis of γένεσις and οὐσία is identical with that of means and end; for a process (and it is in this sense that γένεσις is to be understood) is always for the sake of something other than itself; for example, the building of a ship is for the sake of the ship. Moreover the end, not the means, has intrinsic value, falls under the heading of 'good'. It follows that pleasure, if it is a γένεσις, is not a good. The κομψοί, or rather the κομψός (for he has become singular) 'plainly laughs at those who allege that pleasure is good'.

This conclusion, reached at 54 D, clearly means not merely that pleasure is not *the* good, the sole good or even the chief good, but that it is not *a* good; in fact that 'good' cannot be predicated of any pleasure.[4] Now it is certainly surprising that such a conclusion should be reached, particularly at this stage of the dialogue. For that some pleasures are good is admitted by Socrates at 13 B, and implied at 28 A; and although the pure and true pleasures enumerated at 51 B ff. are not actually called good, it is hardly possible to doubt that Plato regards them as good, and we shall subsequently find them admitted into the mixture which constitutes the good life.

There are two possible solutions of this problem. We may say that it is just another instance of the apparent inconsistency, noted at 52 C,

---

[1] They become a single person afterwards, 54 D.
[2] The αὖ at 53 C6 should be noted.
[3] See Burnet on Aristotle, *E.N.* 1152 B 13, where the phrase occurs.
[4] This cannot indeed be inferred from the use of ἀγαθόν rather than τἀγαθόν at 54 D7; for, as Bury's additional note (p. 215) recognises, the adjective without the article is certainly used for *the* good at 11 B, and possibly also at 13 E; cf. *Rep.* 505 C οἱ τὴν ἡδονὴν ἀγαθὸν ὁριζόμενοι. But the point is settled by the expressions ἡ τοῦ ἀγαθοῦ μοῖρα and ἄλλη μοῖρα (54 C 10–D 2).

between on the one hand calling ἡδονή in general ἄπειρον or ἄμετρον and, on the other, recognising certain ἔμμετροι ἡδοναί and restricting the term 'indefinite' (unlimited) to one kind of pleasures; and we may apply here the explanation offered at p. 102 above. But I am inclined to prefer another solution. Socrates's conclusion is not to be accepted as more than provisional, since its premiss, εἴπερ ἡδονή γένεσίς ἐστιν, is only conditional. But why should Plato trouble to use an argument which rests on a conditional premiss? I would answer, for two reasons: first, that the doctrine of the κομψοί was one that could not be simply ignored in any discussion of pleasure; and secondly, that it can be used to lead to a conclusion less anti-hedonist than that reached at 54 D, a conclusion which Plato can and does fully endorse, which is consonant with his whole attitude to Hedonism both in this dialogue and elsewhere, and which is completely relevant to the main issue. This second and, as we may fairly call it, more reasonable conclusion is drawn at 54 E–55 A: in substance it is this, that man's τέλος—the end with which he can rest satisfied—cannot be found in any pleasure or any sum of pleasures. This is expressed at 54 E, where it is said that the κομψός will laugh at τῶν ἐν ταῖς γενέσεσιν ἀποτελουμένων—a phrase which cannot be adequately translated, for the verb ἀποτελεῖσθαι is given a special meaning which combines the notions of *being perfected* and *finding one's end*. Protarchus needs an explanation; and the explanation which Socrates gives him is, though somewhat abbreviated, intended to recall the argument with Callicles in the *Gorgias* (492–494). To find one's end in pleasure, if pleasure be a γένεσις, is to find it in an unending alternation of γένεσις and φθορά, that is of attainment and loss; the γένεσις is the coming-into-being of a φυσικὴ ἕξις, and the φθορά is the corresponding relapse, without which a recurrence of the γένεσις is impossible.[1]

As the examples of hunger and thirst show, this is no more than a new terminology, in which γένεσις and φθορά replace πλήρωσις and κένωσις. Plato has, in fact, restricted the meaning or application of γένεσις in this last part of his argument, in order to turn the doctrine of the κομψοί to account for the refutation of Philebus, the refutation indeed of all those who find the Good for man in the kind of pleasure which comes under the πλήρωσις-κένωσις formula; and that kind, as we have seen, includes the great majority of the pleasures of sense. The 'pure' pleasures do not come under this formula: for though they are all πληρώσεις, and all therefore involve ἔνδεια or κενότης, they do not involve the cancelling process of κένωσις. Hence those who enjoy them are not of the number of τῶν ἐν ταῖς γενέσεσιν ἀποτελουμένων.[2]

To return to the question of identifying the κομψοί, Aristotle in

---

[1] Compare the use of φθορά and φθείρεσθαι at 31 E, 32 B.

[2] No doubt any πλήρωσις, even the πλήρωσις μαθημάτων, is a process, a γένεσις: but it is not the kind of γένεσις which Plato has here in mind, the γένεσις that implies alternation with φθορά.

E.N. 1152 B 8 ff. distinguishes three types of anti-hedonists, of which the first and third alone concern us here. The first kind hold that no pleasure is good, either in itself or *per accidens*, and their first argument for this is that πᾶσα ἡδονὴ γένεσίς ἐστιν εἰς φύσιν αἰσθητή, οὐδεμία δὲ γένεσις συγγενὴς τοῖς τέλεσιν, οἷον οὐδεμία οἰκοδόμησις οἰκία. Now it seems probable, if we take this argument together with the others ascribed by Aristotle to this first kind of anti-hedonists, that Burnet is right in identifying them with Speusippus and his party. The third kind hold that pleasure is not the chief good (ἄριστον), and their argument is ὅτι οὐ τέλος (*sc.* ἡ ἡδονή ἐστιν) ἀλλὰ γένεσις. Now it is plain that these two arguments are essentially the same as those in the two parts of the section of our dialogue now under discussion; the former is in fact a condensed statement of the first part, with the mere substitution of house-building for ship-building in its illustration; the latter, like the second part of our section, applies the ἡδονή-γένεσις equation not to reach the conclusion that pleasure is not ἀγαθόν, but that it is not ἄριστον. The third kind of anti-hedonists cannot be the party of Speusippus, for their view is much less extreme than his. It seems then reasonable not to identify the κομψοί themselves with Speusippus, but to suppose that someone, whether in the Academy or outside it, put forward an anti-hedonist doctrine to the effect that all pleasure is γένεσις, not οὐσία, without clearly distinguishing the two possible developments of such a doctrine; and that Speusippus developed it in its extreme or radical form, and someone else in its less radical form, both alike drawing upon the present section of our dialogue.[1]

One point remains to be settled. At the end of the section Protarchus says that a number of impossible consequences follow ἐάν τις τὴν ἡδονὴν ὡς ἀγαθὸν ἡμῖν τιθῆται. Does ἀγαθόν *here* stand for τἀγαθόν or not? To say that it does seems best to suit the immediately preceding context, as we have interpreted it; yet we are naturally reluctant to give ἀγαθόν here a different meaning from that which we saw reason to give it in the phrase τῶν φασκόντων ἡδονὴν ἀγαθὸν εἶναι at 54 D 7. It seems, however, necessary to do so, since this speech of Protarchus leads straight on to the following section, in which the improbability of pleasure being the *only* good is the topic. After all, the shift of meaning is not impossible, in view of the fact that since 54 E 1 we have, in effect, been discussing and rejecting the theory that pleasure is the only good, the thesis of Philebus.

Socrates   Protarchus

53 C   *Soc.* And now to pass to another point: are we not told that pleasure is always something that comes to be, that there is no such thing as a pleasure that is? There again[2] you have a theory which certain subtle

---

[1] I am not convinced by Mauersberger's attempt (*Hermes*, LXI, pp. 208 ff.) to identify the κομψοί with the Megarians.

[2] 'Again' (αὖ), as in the case of the 'dour' thinkers of 44 B ff.

thinkers endeavour to expound to us: and we should be grateful to them.

Prot. Why so?

Soc. That is precisely the point which I shall treat at some length in my questions to you, my dear Protarchus.　　　　　　　　　　D

Prot. Pray continue, and put them.

Soc. There are, as you know, two kinds of thing, that which exists independently, and that which is always aiming at something else.

Prot. How do you mean? What are they?

Soc. The one has always pride of place, and the other is its inferior.

Prot. Will you put it still more plainly?

Soc. We have observed before now, I imagine, manly lovers together with the fair and excellent recipients of their admiration?

Prot. To be sure.

Soc. Then see if you can find counterparts to such pairs throughout the world of existence, as we call it.[1]　　　　　　　　　　E

Prot. Must I say yet a third time, 'Please make your meaning plainer, Socrates'?

Soc. It's nothing abstruse, Protarchus; our discussion has been taking a playful turn, but its meaning is that things are always of two kinds, namely those which are with a view to something else, and those for the sake of which the first sort come to be, whenever they do come to be.

Prot. I understand more or less, thanks to your repetitions.

Soc. I daresay we shall understand better before long, my boy, when the argument has made more progress.　　　　　　　　　　54

Prot. No doubt.

Soc. Now let us take another pair.

Prot. Yes?

Soc. All Becoming on the one hand, and all Being on the other.

Prot. I accept your pair, Being and Becoming.

Soc. Very good. Now which of these shall we say is for the sake of which? Becoming for the sake of Being, or Being for the sake of Becoming?

Prot. Are you now enquiring whether what you call Being is what it is for the sake of Becoming?

Soc. Clearly I am.

Prot. Good Heavens! Are you asking me something of this sort: B 'Tell me, Protarchus, do you maintain that shipbuilding goes on for

---

[1] Cf. τῶν ἀεὶ λεγομένων εἶναι, 16 C.

the sake of ships, rather than that ships are for the sake of ship-building?'—and so on and so forth?

Soc. That is precisely what I mean, Protarchus.

Prot. Then why haven't you answered your own question, Socrates?

Soc. I might well do so; but you must take your share in the discussion.

Prot. Yes, certainly.

c   *Soc.* Now I hold that while it is with a view to something coming into being that anyone provides himself with medicine, or tools of any kind, or any sort of material,[1] the becoming always takes place with a view to the being of this or that, so that Becoming in general takes place with a view to Being in general.

Prot. Yes, clearly.

Soc. Then there must be some Being with a view to which pleasure comes to be, if it is true that pleasure is Becoming.

Prot. Of course.

Soc. But where there is this regular relation of means to end, the end falls under the heading of Good; while the means, my excellent friend, must find a place under another heading.

Prot. Most decidedly.

d   *Soc.* Hence if pleasure is Becoming, we shall be right in setting it under some other heading than that of Good?

Prot. Yes, perfectly right.

Soc. And so, as I said at the beginning of our present argument, we ought to be grateful to the author of the doctrine that pleasure is something that comes to be, but in no case ever is; for plainly he laughs to scorn those who assert that pleasure is good.

Prot. Quite so.

e   *Soc.* And what's more, this same thinker will not fail to include in his scorn those who find their satisfaction in these Becomings.

Prot. How do you mean? To whom are you referring?

Soc. To people who, when they find relief for their hunger or thirst

---

[1] Prof. Taylor (*Plato*, p. 428) takes c 1–2 to be still referring to shipbuilding: 'the φάρμακα are, of course, the paints employed for coating the sides of the vessel, etc. So the ὕλη mentioned along with the "tools" does not mean "raw material" in general, but the "timber" from which the planks of the ship are made.' (This is re-affirmed, though less confidently, in his note on *Tim.* 69 A6.) The word πᾶσιν seems to tell strongly against this interpretation: it does not naturally suggest πᾶσι τοῖς ναυπηγοῖς, who have not in fact been mentioned; also we should have expected articles with φάρμακα, πάντα ὄργανα and πᾶσαν ὕλην.

The use of ὕλη for 'raw material' in general is late Greek according to L. and S., who do not quote this passage; but this generalising use in the fourth century would be a natural supposition to account for its technical sense in Aristotle.

or such other troubles as Becoming relieves, are delighted on account of the Becoming, which they regard as a pleasure, saying[1] that they would not care to live without hungering and thirsting and having all the rest of the experiences that might be enumerated as going with hunger and thirst.

Prot. Your description fits them, certainly.   55

Soc. Well now, we should all admit that the opposite of Becoming is Passing away.

Prot. Necessarily.

Soc. Hence it is an alternation[2] of Passing away and Becoming that will be chosen by those who choose a life like that in preference to the third life we spoke of,[3] the life which included neither pleasure nor pain, but the purest possible activity of thought.

Prot. It appears, Socrates, that a number of untenable consequences follow from the proposal to make pleasure our Good.

Soc. Yes: and for that matter we might reinforce the argument.

Prot. How?

55 B–C   *The common-sense attitude towards Hedonism*

This brief section must be treated independently, for it is not part of the development of the doctrine of the κομψοί, but is a direct appeal to common sense against the position of Philebus, that pleasure is the only good. Is it not absurd, asks Socrates, to accept a view which denies all value not only to what are commonly called bodily and external goods, but to the recognised virtues, and which implies that a man is better or worse proportionately to the pleasure and pain which he experiences?

This cannot be intended as a serious refutation of Hedonism. Plato did not suppose that he could thus dispose of Philebus in a few lines.

---

[1] With Callicles, at *Gorgias* 491 E, 494 C.

[2] The argument is abbreviated, for Socrates omits to say that a life which aims at a succession of 'Pleasure-Becomings' must necessarily also aim at a succession of 'Pain-Passings away' (λῦπαι-φθοραί). But Plato's readers would remember this point being made in *Gorgias* 493 D ff., where the life of pleasure is compared to a leaky pitcher.

[3] This is of course the third life in the second triad of lives, not in the first: it is the μέσος βίος of 43 E; and here again, as at 21 E and 33 B, it is associated with the activity of φρόνησις (see above, p. 63). In contrasting it here with the hedonistic life, Socrates does not of course mean that it is the good life for man, but only that it is the polar opposite of the life in which pleasure is constantly alternating with pain; the ideal of Callicles is thus directly opposed to the ideal of Speusippus, but Plato expects his readers to understand, from what has already been said, that the latter ideal is not his own. (I do not imply that Speusippus had necessarily formulated his doctrine when the *Philebus* was written; but it is reasonable to believe that the 'neutral' or 'middle' life was a conception already familiar to the Academy.)

He is really doing no more than indicate the most obvious points of ordinary common-sense belief which Hedonism has to face: it must prove that all the commonly accepted 'goods'—physical beauty and strength, health, noble birth, wealth, fame—as well as knowledge and virtue, are alike valueless. That Plato should be content here with merely pointing this out is quite intelligible; he is not writing this dialogue in order to repeat his own and Socrates's main ethical doctrine; his valuation of external and bodily goods, and of the 'cardinal virtues', has been made sufficiently plain in the early dialogues, and in the *Gorgias* and *Republic*. He has in fact abundantly refuted Hedonism long ago, most fully and directly perhaps in the *Gorgias*; why should he now repeat the discussion between Socrates and Callicles, even if Protarchus were (as he is not) cast for the rôle in question?[1] The purpose of our dialogue is not to refute the doctrine that pleasure is the only good, although it is Plato's intention that throughout the discussion that doctrine should be at the back of his readers' minds, even as Philebus is lying 'back-stage' (15 c) all through the dialogue. It is because that is not the purpose of the dialogue that it starts by merely recording the fact that Philebus has maintained his thesis, and forthwith raises, in discussion between Socrates and Protarchus (who is not really the Hedonist that he fancies himself to be), the main question, namely what place must be assigned to pleasure in the good life, and what sorts of pleasure can there find admission.

But it is perfectly natural, and dramatically right, that our present section should stand where it does, if only we understand Plato's real intention in it. We are about to undertake the classification of knowledge, and before we do so it is well that we should be reminded that, although knowledge is (as was agreed at 14 B and will be repeated in a moment at 55 c) to be treated in the same way as pleasure in so far as its various forms are to be discriminated and graded in value, yet it has long since been vindicated as *a* good, and has not now to establish its claim to be an ingredient of the good life, but only its superior value in that good life to such pleasures as *can* establish their claim to belong to that ἕξις ψυχῆς καὶ διάθεσις which constitutes Happiness.

| Socrates | Protarchus |

55 B   *Soc.* Surely it is untenable that there should be nothing good nor admirable in our bodies, nor yet in anything else whatever except in our souls,[2] and that there it should be pleasure alone that is good, not

---

[1] It is true that he has reminded us of that discussion, and has dealt directly with the position of Philebus, in the last section (53 c–55 A); but, as I have argued, that section is in the nature of an appendix.

[2] This is perhaps the clearest indication in the dialogue that pleasure and pain are psychical, not bodily, experiences, though they may originate in the body. This has been implied at least since 35 D. Cf. τὸ δὲ τὴν ἀλγηδόνα ἤ τινα διὰ πάθος ἡδονὴν τὸ σῶμα ἦν τὸ παρεχόμενον, 41 C.

courage nor temperance nor reason nor any of the goods proper to
soul—these being no good at all? And, what is more, that one who
feels not pleasure, but distress, should be forced to admit that every
time he feels distress he is evil, though he be in fact the best of men,
and conversely that one who feels pleasure should gain an additional
excellence proportionate to his pleasure, every time he feels that pleasure. c
Prot. The whole idea, Socrates, is as untenable as it well could be.

55 C–59 C   *Classification of forms of knowledge*

We now proceed to discover distinctions, in respect of purity and
'mixedness' within knowledge, corresponding to those already discovered within pleasure. The general principle of distinction is the
same as that which determines the selection of propaedeutic studies in
Rep. VII, namely the presence or absence of mathematical methods in
the procedure of a science. Just as there the mathematical sciences
were held worthy of study by the Guardians as a preliminary to the
μέγιστον μάθημα of dialectic, so here the 'arts' of numbering, measuring
and weighing are pronounced to be the leading or principal arts[1]
(ἡγεμονικάς 55 D, πρώτας 56 C), save for dialectic, whose paramount
position is dwelt on at length. Dialectic alone is declared to have as its
object true changeless Being, and therefore to 'have more hold on
truth' (τῆς ἀληθείας ἀντέχεσθαι μᾶλλον, 58 E) than any other science or
art. Whatever view be taken about the objects of the two highest
segments of the Line in *Rep.* VI–VII, it seems clear that now not only
are the mathematical sciences, as before, of less value than dialectic,
but their objects too are lower.[2]

Plato seeks to emphasise the paramount position of dialectic as the
science of true Being by contrasting it with rhetoric, which Protarchus,
as a disciple of Gorgias, is inclined to think 'far the best' of all the
arts (58 B). Socrates, in answering him, discloses an attitude towards
rhetoric very different from his contemptuous attitude in the *Gorgias*;
he is ready to concede the greatest practical value to this art (we hear
no more of such expressions as ἄτεχνος τριβή[3]); and it is clearly implied

[1] The word τέχνη alternates with ἐπιστήμη throughout these pages, but when
it is inappropriate Plato sometimes (e.g. 57 D) uses the feminine adjectives,
ἀριθμητική etc., alone, as Greek idiom permits: 'philosophic' arithmetic is not
a τέχνη. When dialectic comes into the picture the word γνῶσις appears (58 A);
yet even at 58 E we have ἐπιστήμην ἢ τέχνην, though here perhaps ἢ should be
regarded as fully disjunctive (*aut*).

[2] The passage indicates, perhaps more clearly than any other in the dialogues,
at least an approach to the doctrine of 'intermediate mathematical objects'
ascribed to Plato by Aristotle at *Met.* 987 B 15 and elsewhere.

[3] Already in the *Phaedrus* (though Taylor, *Plato*, p. 319, may be right in saying
that that dialogue 'modifies nothing that was said' (sc. about rhetoric) 'in the
earlier dialogue') the tone is very different. Great value is accorded to a reformed,
scientific rhetoric, and this is assimilated to medicine at 270 B, instead of being
contrasted with it. Cf. also *Pol.* 304 A.

that utility (χρεία, ὠφελία) is not claimed for dialectic, whose supreme position rests solely on its truth, in other words on its cognition of true Being. This is noteworthy as an approach towards the Aristotelian conception of θεωρητικὴ ἐπιστήμη, as indicated in such passages as *Met.* 982 A 14 καὶ τῶν ἐπιστημῶν δὲ τὴν αὐτῆς ἕνεκεν καὶ τοῦ εἰδέναι χάριν αἱρετὴν οὖσαν μᾶλλον εἶναι σοφίαν ἢ τὴν τῶν ἀποβαινόντων ἕνεκεν, 982 B 20 φανερὸν ὅτι διὰ τὸ εἰδέναι τὸ ἐπίστασθαι ἐδίωκον καὶ οὐ χρήσεώς τινος ἕνεκεν.[1]

Another feature which recalls the *Republic* is the distinction here drawn between the 'philosophic' and 'non-philosophic' sorts of arithmetic and geometry (57 C–D), or the 'philosophic' and 'industrial and commercial' (56 E). In the *Republic*, however, the distinction is not so sharp: it is in fact a distinction of *purposes* rather than of sciences: e.g. at 525 B–C the Guardians must ἐπὶ λογιστικὴν ἰέναι...οὐκ ὠνῆς οὐδὲ πράσεως χάριν ὡς ἐμπόρους ἢ καπήλους μελετῶντας, ἀλλ' ἕνεκα πολέμου τε καὶ αὐτῆς τῆς ψυχῆς ῥαστώνης μεταστροφῆς ἀπὸ γενέσεως ἐπ' ἀλήθειάν τε καὶ οὐσίαν.

The general purport of this section is plain enough, but the structure of the argument is difficult. The chief trouble is this: the 'leading' arts or sciences, which we are bidden to pick out at 55 D 10, appear at first not to be independent sciences at all, but methods or factors within certain sciences; then at 56 A–C we get a dichotomy into two groups of arts, of which τεκτονική and μουσική respectively are the typical representatives. The *fundamentum divisionis* is employment of numeration, measurement, or weighing; yet immediately after the dichotomy has been formally announced (56 C 4–6) we are faced with a third group, consisting of precisely these three 'arts'—numeration, measurement and weighing—and these are declared to be more exact than any others (ἀκριβεστάτας), and also to be the 'primary' (πρώτας) arts spoken of 'just now', which appears to mean that they are (as indeed we have expected all along) the 'leading arts' referred to at 55 D 10.

In addition to this seeming confusion, the whole classification begins with a dichotomy of τῆς περὶ τὰ μαθήματα ἐπιστήμης into τὸ δημιουργικόν and τὸ περὶ παιδείαν καὶ τροφήν, but of the latter species we hear no more, *eo nomine*, in the sequel.

The clue to these puzzles is probably this, that Plato, the ἐραστὴς διαιρέσεων (*Phaedr.* 266 B, cf. *Phil.* 16 B–C), has forced into the mould of logical division a classification of arts or sciences which are not, in fact, co-ordinate species of a genus, but whose relation is one of greater or less approximation to truth (ἀλήθεια) or precision (ἀκρίβεια). If this suggestion be right, it becomes easy to understand that one 'species'

---

[1] The notion of θεωρία—the contemplation of truth for its own sake—does not of course now for the first time make its appearance in Plato; it is, for example, clearly present in the *Theaetetus* 'digression' (172 C ff.). But in the main Plato has hitherto thought of dialectic as an instrument not only for attaining truth, but for knowing the Good and using that knowledge as a statesman may use it. This is the leading thought at least in the *Republic*.

or group of arts can contain within itself, as an element in itself, another 'species'; what is really meant is that there is more true science in some 'sciences' or arts than in others. But διαίρεσις is an unreal and confusing procedure for expressing this simple idea.

The lowest group (μουσική etc.[1]), whose procedure is just 'rule of thumb' (or rather of finger and ear), has little or no ἀκρίβεια; the next group (τεκτονική etc.) uses measuring instruments and has much; third, and higher still, come the arts of measuring, numbering etc. themselves, and these are ἀκριβέσταται (56 c 8). But this having been said, a qualification has at once to be made: for it is not the kind of numbering etc. that we have hitherto been necessarily thinking of—the counting of concrete things, the measurement of spatial objects with a foot-rule, in short all the applied mathematics used in the manual arts (τὸ δημιουργικόν)—that can claim absolute ἀκρίβεια. That can only belong to the 'philosophic' calculation or measurement which, unlike that of the builder and trader, operates with equal units (56 D–E).

On this point there will be more to be said in a moment. But meantime let us realise that with this fourth type of science (the word 'art' has now become inappropriate) we have got out of the region of τὸ δημιουργικόν altogether; we have, so to speak, overleapt the troublesome barrier of an unreal διαίρεσις; or alternatively, if we prefer to believe that the original dichotomy is still in Plato's mind, we may say that we have now passed, though without mentioning it, to the other species of that dichotomy, viz. to τὸ περὶ παιδείαν καὶ τροφήν: we are in fact in the region of the προπαιδεία of *Rep.* VII.

Fifth, and highest of all, comes dialectic: and to this Plato does not give even a semblance of belonging to the διαίρεσις scheme. Looked at from the standpoint of the original division of 55 D 1–3, it might doubtless be said to be part of τὸ περὶ παιδείαν καὶ τροφήν: but nothing is said of its educative value, and since the *fundamentum divisionis* hitherto employed—the possession of greater or less ἀκρίβεια due to the presence or absence of mathematical procedure—is here inapplicable, it is best to think of dialectic as *sui generis* in Plato's mind, as it is in fact.

To return to the question of the equal units of 'philosophical arithmetic': here again Plato is making the same point as in *Rep.* 525 D–526 A, that no arithmetical operation can be exact unless its units be precisely equal. No doubt it is true, for practical purposes, that one fat ox added to one lean ox makes two oxen; but it is not mathematically true, for the weight and volume of the total is not double the weight and volume either of the first ox or of the second; in other words, the real meaning or implication of $1 + 1 = 2$ is not exemplified in the concrete case. Nor indeed could it be in any concrete case, since

---

[1] μουσική might perhaps have been expected to come under τὸ περὶ παιδείαν καὶ τροφήν: but cf. *Pol.* 304 B μουσικῆς ἐστι πού τις ἡμῖν μάθησις, καὶ ὅλως τῶν περὶ χειροτεχνίας ἐπιστημῶν;

(as was pointed out at *Phaedo* 74 B) no two physical objects are ever precisely equal. The truths of mathematics are approximately, but never fully, represented in the world of sense.[1]

Socrates   Protarchus

55 C   *Soc.* Well now, we have been trying every possible method of reviewing pleasure: but don't let us show ourselves over-tender towards reason and knowledge. Rather let us test their metal with a good honest ring, to see if it contains any base alloy; for by so doing we shall detect what is really the purest element in them, and so use, for the purpose of our joint decision, their truest parts together with the truest parts of pleasure.

Prot. Right.

D   *Soc.* Now we may, I think, divide the knowledge involved in our studies into technical knowledge, and that concerned with education and culture; may we not?

Prot. Yes.

Soc. Then taking the technical knowledge employed in handicraft, let us first consider whether one division is more closely concerned with knowledge, and the other less so,[2] so that we are justified in regarding the first kind as the purest, and the second as relatively impure.

Prot. Yes, we ought so to regard them.

Soc. Should we then mark off the superior types of knowledge in the several crafts?[3]

Prot. How so? Which do you mean?

E   *Soc.* If, for instance, from any craft you subtract the element of

---

[1] The point is clearly explained by J. S. Mill, quoted by Grote, *Plato*, II, p. 66: 'In all propositions concerning numbers a condition is implied without which none of them would be true, and that condition is an assumption which may be false. The condition is that $1 = 1$: that all the numbers are numbers of the same or equal units. Let this be doubtful, and not one of the propositions in arithmetic will hold true. How can we know that one pound and one pound make two pounds, if one of the pounds be troy and the other avoirdupois? They may not make two pounds of either or of any weight....One actual pound weight is not exactly equal to another, nor one mile's length to another; a nicer balance or more exact measuring instruments would always detect some difference.'

[2] I accept Schleiermacher's ἐστί for ἔνι in D 6. There is a slight illogicality of expression in this sentence, for ἐπιστήμαις must be understood with ταῖς χειροτεχνικαῖς, and there cannot be a closer adherence to ἐπιστήμη in some ἐπιστῆμαι than in others. But the reason for this illogicality will be apparent from what has been said about the structure of the whole argument.

[3] τὰς ἡγεμονικὰς (sc. ἐπιστήμας) in D 10 means the same as τὸ ἐπιστήμης μᾶλλον ἐχόμενον above, and ἑκάστων αὐτῶν (which is not governed by χωρίς) means 'in each of the χειροτεχνικαὶ ἐπιστῆμαι'.

numbering, measuring, and weighing, the remainder will be almost negligible.

Prot. Negligible indeed.

Soc. For after doing so, what you would have left would be guesswork and the exercise of your senses on a basis of experience and rule of thumb, involving the use of that ability to make lucky shots which is commonly accorded the title of art or craft, when it has consolidated its position by dint of industrious practice.   56

Prot. I have not the least doubt you are right.

Soc. Well now, we find plenty of it, to take one instance, in music when it adjusts its concords not by measurement but by lucky shots of a practised finger; in the whole of music, flute-playing and lyre-playing alike,[1] for this latter hunts for the proper length of each string as it gives its note,[2] making a shot for the note, and attaining a most unreliable result with a large element of uncertainty.

Prot. Very true.

Soc. Then again we shall find the same sort of thing in medicine and B agriculture and navigation and military science.

Prot. Quite so.

Soc. Building, however, makes a considerable use of measures and instruments, and the remarkable exactness thus attained makes it more scientific than most sorts of knowledge.

Prot. In what respect?

Soc. I am thinking of the building of ships and houses, and various other uses to which timber is put. It employs straight-edge and peg- C and-cord, I believe, and compasses and plummet, and an ingenious kind of set-square.

Prot. You are perfectly right, Socrates.

Soc. Let us then divide the arts and crafts so-called[3] into two classes, those akin to music in their activities and those akin to carpentry, the two classes being marked by a lesser and a greater degree of exactness respectively.

Prot. So be it.

Soc. And let us take those arts, which just now we spoke of as primary,[4] to be the most exact of all.

[1] I accept the addition of καὶ κιθαριστική after αὐλητική, given by the second hand in Ven., and take αὐτῆς as = τῆς στοχαστικῆς and as governed by μεστή.

[2] In 56 A 6 φερομένης gives no sense, and I accept Badham's φθεγγομένης. For φθέγγεσθαι of a lyre, cf. *Rep.* 531 A, Ar. *Met.* 1019 B 15.

[3] 'So-called' because the first kind do not deserve the name: cf. τέχνας ἐπονομάζουσι above (56 A 1).

[4] A loose reference to the 'leading types of knowledge' of 55 D.

Prot. I take it you mean the art of numbering, and the others which you mentioned in association with it just now.

D *Soc.* To be sure. But ought we not, Protarchus, to recognise these themselves to be of two kinds? What do you think?

Prot. What two kinds do you mean?

Soc. To take first numbering or arithmetic, ought we not to distinguish between that of the ordinary man and that of the philosopher?

Prot. On what principle, may I ask, is this discrimination of two arithmetics to be based?

Soc. There is an important mark of difference, Protarchus. The ordinary arithmetician, surely, operates with unequal units: his 'two' may be two armies or two cows or two anythings from the smallest thing in the world to the biggest; while the philosopher will have

E nothing to do with him, unless he consents to make every single instance of his unit precisely equal to every other of its infinite number of instances.

Prot. Certainly you are right in speaking of an important distinction amongst those who concern themselves with number, which justifies the belief that there are two arithmetics.

Soc. Then as between the calculating and measurement employed in building or commerce and the geometry and calculation practised

57 in philosophy—well, should we say there is one sort of each, or should we recognise two sorts?

Prot. On the strength of what has been said[1] I should give my vote for there being two.

Soc. Right. Now do you realise our purpose in bringing these matters on to the board?

Prot. Possibly, but I should like you to pronounce on the point.

Soc. Well, it seems to me that our discussion, now no less than when we embarked upon it, has propounded a question here analogous to the question about pleasures:[2] it is enquiring whether one kind of

B knowledge is purer than another, just as one pleasure is purer than another.

Prot. Yes, it is quite clear that that has been its reason for attacking this matter.

---

[1] It seems necessary to read τοῖς, with Bekker and Bury, for τῇ in 57 A 3. So Apelt, 'Auf Grund des Bisherigen'.

[2] Some emendation of the text seems necessary here, but Apelt's προβεβληκέναι σκοπόν does not seem to me a possible expression. The easiest remedy seems to be ζήτησιν for ζητῶν (Stephens: see Bury's note).

Soc. Well now, in what preceded had it not discovered that different arts, dealing with different things, possessed different degrees of precision? *Prot.* Certainly.

Soc. And in what followed did it not first mention a certain art under one single name, making us think it really was one art, and then treat it as two, putting questions about the precision and purity of c those two to find out whether the art as practised by the philosopher or by the non-philosopher was the more exact? *Prot.* I certainly think that is the question which it puts.

Soc. Then, Protarchus, what answer do we give it?

Prot. We have got far enough, Socrates, to discern an astonishingly big difference between one kind of knowledge and another in respect of precision.

Soc. Well, will that make it easier for us to answer?

Prot. Of course; and let our statement be that the arts which we have had before us are superior to all others, and that those amongst them which involve the effort of the true philosopher are, in their use of D measure and number, immensely superior in point of exactness and truth.

Soc. Let it be as you put it; then relying on you we shall confidently answer the clever twisters of argument[1]—

Prot. Answer what?

Soc. That there are two arts of numbering and two arts of measuring, and plenty of other kindred arts which are similarly pairs of twins, though they share a single name.

Prot. Let us give that answer, Socrates, with our blessing to those E clever folk, as you style them.

Soc. Then these are the kinds of knowledge which we maintain to be pre-eminently exact?

Prot. Certainly.

Soc. But we, Protarchus, are likely to be repudiated by the art of dialectic, if we prefer any other to her.

Prot. Then how ought we to describe her, in her turn?

Soc. Plainly everyone will recognise her whom we now speak of.[2] 58 The cognition of that which is, that which exists in reality,[3] ever

---

[1] These are the same sort of people as those who, at *Rep.* 454 A, fall into τὴν ἀντιλογικὴν τέχνην because they cannot κατ' εἴδη διαιρούμενοι τὸ λεγόμενον ἐπισκοπεῖν It is a common failing, and no particular school or sect is alluded to.

[2] The words τὴν γε νῦν λεγομένην may imply that there are two kinds of τὸ διαλέγεσθαι, 'dialectic' and mere conversation.

[3] I bracket τὸ before κατὰ ταὐτόν.

unchanged, is held, I cannot doubt, by all people who have the smallest endowment of reason to be far and away truer than any other. What is your view? How would you, Protarchus, decide about this question?

Prot. On the many occasions when I used to listen to Gorgias, he regularly said, Socrates, that the art of persuasion was greatly superior
B to all others, for it subjugated all things not by violence but by willing submission, and was far and away the best of all arts: but on this occasion I should not care to take up a position against either you or him.

Soc. 'Take up arms' I fancy you meant to say, but you dropped them out of modesty.

Prot. Well, have it as you choose.

Soc. I wonder if I am to blame for your misconception.

Prot. What is it?

Soc. What I wanted to discover at present, my dear Protarchus, was
C not which art or which form of knowledge is superior to all others in respect of being the greatest or the best or the most serviceable, but which devotes its attention to precision, exactness, and the fullest truth,[1] though it may be small and of small profit: that is what we are looking for at this moment. What you must consider—and you won't give offence to Gorgias, if you allow his art the property of doing paramount service to mankind, while assigning to the procedure to which I have just referred just that property of possessing paramount truth which I illustrated by showing that a small quantity of pure
D white colour was superior to a large quantity of impure in that respect— what you must consider is, whether the art we have in mind may reasonably be said to possess in fullest measure reason and intelligence in their purity, or whether we ought to look for some other art with a better claim. The question calls for great thought and ample reflexion, and we must have no regard for any benefits a science may confer or any repute it may enjoy; but if there is a certain faculty in our souls naturally directed to loving truth and doing all for the sake of truth, let us make diligent search and say what it is; and when we have done so you must consider the question I have put to you.[2]

E *Prot.* Well, I have been thinking it over, and in my opinion it

---

[1] Is Aristotle implicitly criticising the suggestion here made, that the truest science may not be the best, when he writes ἀναγκαιότεραι μὲν οὖν πᾶσαι ταύτης (i.e. σοφίας), ἀμείνων δ' οὐδεμία (*Met.* 983 A 10)?

[2] In this long sentence (c 5–D 8) Plato allows Socrates' fervour to break loose from the restraints of formal grammar at several points. Translation demands some such rearrangement of clauses as I have attempted, as well as the substitution of a more normal structure.

would be difficult to concede that any other science or art has more of a hold on truth than this one.

Soc. Now does it occur to you, in saying what you have just said, that the majority of arts, as also those who are busied therewith, are in the first place concerned with opinions and pursue their energetic 59 studies in the realm of opinion? And are you aware that those of them who do consider themselves students of reality spend a whole lifetime in studying the universe around us, how it came to be, how it does things and how things happen to it?[1] May we say that is so? What do you think?

Prot. We may.

Soc. Then the task which such students amongst us have taken upon themselves has nothing to do with that which always is, but only with what is coming into being, or will come, or has come.

Prot. Very true.

Soc. And can we say that any precise and exact truth attaches to things, none of which are at this present, or ever were, or ever will be ʀ free from change?

Prot. Of course not.

Soc. And how can we ever get a permanent grasp on anything that is entirely devoid of permanence?

Prot. Nohow, I imagine.

Soc. It follows then that reason too, and knowledge that gives perfect truth, are foreign to them.

Prot. So it would seem.

Soc. Then we should have done for good and all with your illustrious self, and mine, and with Gorgias and Philebus,[2] and make the following reasoned declaration:

---

[1] The language suggests a personal allusion, and it is not impossible that Plato is thinking of Democritus. The attitude to cosmology, and to physical science in general, is fully consonant with that of the *Timaeus*, where the account of the κόσμος is declared (29 B–D) to be no more than an εἰκὼς μῦθος because the universe is a γιγνόμενον—a thing not of stable being, but of perpetual becoming. Yet in so far as the physical world manifests the eternal Reason and Goodness to which it owes its existence, its study is worth while; if it were not, Plato would not have troubled to write the *Timaeus*. What is not, in his view, worth while is a materialist or mechanistic account of the universe, which by conceiving it *merely* as γένεσις, or (as he would put it) by discovering the work of ἀνάγκη and omitting that of νοῦς, fails to give even an εἰκὼς μῦθος, because it ignores the fact that the γιγνόμενον is an εἰκὼς of the ὄν. (On this 'obvious connexion of εἰκὼς with εἰκών' see some excellent remarks by Mr J. B. Skemp in his recent work, *The Theory of Motion in Plato's Later Dialogues*, p. 67.)

[2] The personal controversy has disappeared under the cogency of impersonal reasoning.

H P   Q

c   *Prot.* Let us have it.

Soc. That we find fixity, purity, truth and what we have called
perfect clarity, either in those things that are always, unchanged,
unaltered and free of all admixture,[1] or in what is most akin[2] to them;
everything else must be called inferior and of secondary importance.

59 C–61 C   *Recapitulation of earlier conclusions about the Good Life*
             It is a good mixture, but in what does its goodness consist?

The discussion can now revert to the original question of the Good
Life. It was settled long ago (22 A) that this must be a mixture of
pleasure and intelligence; and now that we have investigated the
various kinds of pleasure and intelligence, and found that some are
truer and purer than others, we realise that we must secure a *good*
mixture: in other words, not any and every compound of these
ingredients is good.

Socrates arrives at this conclusion at 61 A, after a recapitulation of
earlier conclusions as to the insufficiency of either of the 'unmixed
lives'. He reminds us that we asked which life might properly be
awarded the second prize, and says that to determine this we must
know what 'the good' (τὸ ἀγαθόν) is, in outline at least.

It is of the first importance that we should grasp what this means.
This is one of those places where a technical philosophical terminology
would have made Plato's meaning clearer; but as usual he has preferred
to avoid this, and keeps to the language of ordinary conversation.
There is, however, no real obscurity, for instead of philosophical
'jargon' we are given an illuminating metaphor. We have, says
Socrates, discovered the *residence* of τὸ ἀγαθόν: that residence is the
mixed life, or rather (as he immediately adds, 61 B 8) the well-mixed
life; and if we have found the residence, we are well on the way to
finding the resident. Plainly this means that we have still to discover
not τὸ ἀγαθόν in the sense of something to which the predicate 'good'
can be properly assigned, but αὐτὸ τὸ ἀγαθόν, goodness itself, the
universal. And by saying that we may hope to find this in what is
well-mixed, Socrates means that it must be not any ingredient of the

---

[1] The μεῖξις here denied of the Ideas is of course not the μεῖξις of πέρας and
ἄπειρον, but something quite different. Nevertheless it may be doubted whether
Plato would have used this phrase τὰ ἀεί... ἀμεικτότατα ἔχοντα if he had intended,
as some scholars believe, to include the Ideas in the μεικτὸν γένος of 23 c ff.

[2] In the light of *Timaeus*, *Laws* VII, X and XII, and *Epinomis* (if it be genuine,
as I believe) it is safe to say that Plato is alluding to the subject-matter of
astronomy. Truth, purity and fixity belong to it because its objects, though not
eternal, like the Forms, in their own right, are yet everlasting unities of soul and
body because their Creator has willed that they should be (*Tim.* 41 B); in these
'created gods' the beneficent purpose of the Cosmic Mind has its fullest and
most perfect fulfilment. Cf. *Laws* VII, 821 A, where astronomy is called καλὸν καὶ
ἀληθὲς μάθημα καὶ πόλει συμφέρον καὶ τῷ θεῷ παντάπασι φίλον.

mixture, but the *form* of the mixture.¹ Yet we shall do well to bear in mind that perhaps only an 'outline' of the Good is possible (61 A 4).

It is apparent from this passage alone that Plato would fully agree with Prof. G. E. Moore that 'this question, how "good" is to be defined, is the most fundamental question in all Ethics'.²

The distinction between *what is good* and goodness (*what good is*) has not now for the first time emerged, though it is only now that it is made prominent. At 22 B Socrates said that neither of the unmixed lives 'proves to *contain* the good' (δῆλον ὡς οὐδέτερος· αὐτοῖν εἶχε τἀγαθόν), and at 22 D he spoke of 'that, whatever it is, which by its inclusion makes that life both desirable and good' (ὅτι ποτ' ἔστι τοῦτο ὃ λαβὼν ὁ βίος οὖτος γέγονεν αἱρετὸς ἅμα καὶ ἀγαθός). In this latter passage ὃ λαβὼν is equivalent to οὗ μεταλαβὼν, and indicates the 'participation' of the good life in the Form of Goodness.

It might perhaps be thought that we have already discovered what goodness is in the discussion of the ἕτερα βέλη (23 B–31 A). It was there shown that there is a Cosmic Mind which is the author (efficient cause) of all 'right association' of Limit and Unlimited. But this Mind is not identified with goodness, any more than the Demiurge of the *Timaeus* is identified with his παράδειγμα, the νοητὸν ζῷον. The truth seems to be that Plato never states, save in this metaphor of the artist and his model, the relation between the two entities which are both essential to his metaphysic, namely the independently existing Form of the Good and the spiritual being—God—who is himself perfectly good. The universe, so far as it is good, is so because it 'partakes' of goodness, and it is God (νοῦς) who causes it to partake thereof.

Neoplatonism did attempt to state this relation in precise terms; but it may be doubted whether Plotinus's derivation of νοῦς from the One (the Good) is any real improvement on Plato's metaphor. He may have shown that logic forces us to postulate the Supreme One, a more ultimate entity than νοῦς, but he no more than Plato can explain, otherwise than by metaphors of emanation or radiation, *how* the second Hypostasis proceeds from the first.

The recognition of the need for a Mind as the efficient cause of the Good in the Universe was, it would seem, late in Plato's philosophical development. In *Sophist* 248 E he acknowledges through the mouth of the Eleatic Stranger, in language which manifestly reveals a new illumination, that reality cannot consist of nothing but the static Forms, but must include Life, Soul and Mind. This was the beginning of Plato's theism, as distinct from his criticism of current theology, and thenceforward theism is prominent in his writings: in *Timaeus*, *Philebus*, *Politicus* (the myth) and the metaphysical books of *Laws* (x and the latter part of XII). It is a complement to, not a substitute for,

---

¹ I do not, of course, imply that Plato now, any more than at any other time, regards Forms as mere *universalia in re*.

² *Principia Ethica*, § 5.

nor yet a reformed version of, the Theory of Ideas; but the two factors
of his ontology are left imperfectly adjusted in his writings: though
it does not follow that it was so in his own mind, for their adjustment
would doubtless be one of those matters of which he wrote in Epistle VII
(341 D) that they are not γραπτέα ἱκανῶς πρὸς τοὺς πολλοὺς καὶ ῥητά.

Protarchus   Socrates

59 C   *Prot.* What you say is very true.

Soc. Then as regards names for what we have been discussing, will
it not be fittest to assign the fairest names to the fairest things?

Prot. I suppose so.

D   *Soc.* And are not Reason and Intelligence the names that command
the greatest respect?

Prot. Yes.

Soc. Then these names can be properly established in usage as
precisely appropriate to thought whose object is true Being.[1]

Prot. Certainly.

Soc. But I may point out that it was just these names about which
I originally suggested that we had to make our decision.

Prot. To be sure, Socrates.

Soc. Very well. Then here, one may say, we have at hand the
E   ingredients, intelligence and pleasure, ready to be mixed: the materials
in which, or out of which, we as builders are to build our structure:
that would not be a bad metaphor.

Prot. Quite a good one.

Soc. Next then, I suppose. we must set to work to mix them.

Prot. Of course.

Soc. I suggest that there are points which we might do well to
remind ourselves of first.

[1] This restriction of the terms νοῦς and φρόνησις to cognition of the highest
reality is unexpected. Hitherto both words, and ἐπιστήμη as well, have been used
in a wide sense, and to all appearance synonymously. φρόνησις has very often
been thus used alone (e.g. 12 A, 14 B, 20 B, E, 27 C, D): at other times it has been
coupled with νοῦς (e.g. 22 A, 28 D). A comparison of 20 A6 with B7 shows the
equivalence of ἐπιστήμη and φρόνησις. The threefold expression φρόνησίς τε καὶ
ἐπιστήμη καὶ νοῦς is used at 13 E, and φρόνησιν καὶ νοῦν καὶ ἐπιστήμην καὶ μνήμην
πᾶσαν at 21 D. Nor is the narrower meaning now introduced always adhered to
in the remaining pages of the dialogue; for a comparison of 61 D 1 and D 10 shows
that φρόνησις is again interchangeable with ἐπιστήμη, while at 65 D9 the collocation νοῦ καὶ ἐπιστήμης, following upon an uncoupled φρόνησις at D 5, strongly
suggests that the three are again synonymous. Nevertheless Plato probably does
wish a special dignity to be attached to νοῦς and φρόνησις, and this will reappear
in the fivefold classification of goods at 66 A ff., where ἐπιστῆμαι occupy a lower
place than the other two.

Prot. What are they?

Soc. Points we mentioned before; but I think there is a lot in the proverb about the need for repeating a good thing 'once and twice 60 and once again'.

Prot. To be sure.

Soc. Come along, then, I beg and beseech you: I think I can give you the gist of what we said.

Prot. Yes?

Soc. Philebus maintains that pleasure is the proper quest of all living creatures, and that all ought to aim at it; in fact he says that the Good for all is pleasure and nothing else, these two terms, pleasure and good, being properly applied to one thing, one single existent. Socrates on the other hand maintains that they are not one thing, but two, in fact B as in name: 'good' and 'pleasant' are different from one another, and intelligence has more claim to be ranked as good than pleasure. Are not those the assertions, Protarchus, now as before?

Prot. Exactly.

Soc. And is there not a further point on which we should agree, now as then?

Prot. What is that?

Soc. That the Good differs from everything else in a certain respect.

Prot. In what respect?   c

Soc. A creature that possesses it permanently, completely and absolutely, has never any need of anything else; its satisfaction is perfect. Is that right?

Prot. Yes, that is right.

Soc. And we went on, by way of experiment, to imagine the individual lives corresponding to them when each was isolated from the other: that of pleasure unmixed with intelligence, and that of intelligence similarly devoid of any particle of pleasure.

Prot. We did.

Soc. And did we find that either of them was satisfactory to anybody?

Prot. No indeed.   D

Soc. But if we made any slip before, now is the time for anyone[1] who likes to take the matter up and restate it more correctly. Let him class together memory, intelligence, knowledge and true opinion, and ask himself whether there is anything whatever that he would choose

---

[1] Anyone, that is, of the company present, which includes others besides the three speakers (16 A, 19 c).

to have, or to get, without these: anything, let alone a pleasure which, for all its magnitude or extreme intensity, he felt without any true opinion that he felt it, without any recognition whatever of the
E character of his experience, without even a momentary memory of it. And then let him put the same question about intelligence, whether anyone would choose to have intelligence unaccompanied by any pleasure, even of the most fleeting character, in preference to its accompaniment by some: [or to have every pleasure without any intelligence in preference to its accompaniment by some].[1]

Prot. Impossible, Socrates: there is no need to put that question more than once.

61   *Soc.* Then neither of the two can be the perfect thing that everyone desires, the absolute Good.

Prot. No.

Soc. Then we shall have to grasp the Good, either precisely or at least in rough outline, if we are to know to what we must give, as we put it, the second prize.

Prot. You are quite right.

Soc. And haven't we in a sense found a way towards the Good?

Prot. How?

Soc. If you were looking for somebody and began by ascertaining
B correctly where he lived, I imagine that would be a big step towards discovering the man you looked for.

Prot. Of course.

Soc. Well, so it is here: our discussion has made it plain to us, now as at the outset, that we must not look for the Good in the unmixed life, but in the mixed.[2]

Prot. Quite so.

Soc. But there is more hope of what we are looking for coming to light in what is well mixed than in what is badly mixed?

---

[1] The sentence is complete with the words μετά τινων ἡδονῶν, and what follows is an otiose and illogical repetition of the substance of D 7–E 1; it may well be a spurious addition.
[2] The language here is perhaps deliberately ambiguous: the recommendation to seek for τὸ ἀγαθόν in the Mixed Life could mean that the Mixed Life *is* τὸ ἀγαθόν, as in one sense of τὸ ἀγαθόν it is. But Socrates's previous words (A 9–B 2) should have made it clear that we are to look behind this for the *goodness* in the Mixed Life, for the immanent character whereby it participates in the Form of Goodness itself. This is treated in the sequel as equivalent to seeking for αὐτὸ τὸ ἀγαθόν, though strictly, no doubt, Plato thinks (as at *Phaedo* 102 D, 103 B; *Parm.* 130 B) of the transcendent Form and the immanent character as distinct. (On this point see Cornford, *Plato and Parmenides*, p. 78.)

Prot. Much more.

Soc. Then let us mingle our ingredients, Protarchus, with a prayer to the gods, to Dionysus or Hephaestus or whichever god has been c assigned this function of mingling.

Prot. By all means.

Soc. Why, it's just as if we were supplying drinks, with two fountains at our disposal: one would be of honey, standing for pleasure; the other, standing for intelligence, a sobering, unintoxicating fountain of plain, salubrious water; we must get to work and make a really good mixture.

Prot. Of course.

61 D–64 A   *What kinds of knowledge and of pleasure are admissible in the Good Life?*

We now proceed to select the ingredients of the mixture. First as to knowledge, we must of course have the 'truest part' of this, namely the knowledge of true, immutable Being; but it is agreed that an inferior kind must be included as well; in fact we shall allow any and every sort of intellectual activity ('all the knowledges', πάσας τὰς ἐπιστήμας) a place.

This decision is taken out of regard for the needs of practical life. We could not build a house in the light of pure mathematics alone; in manipulating sensible objects, bricks and mortar and so forth, we must employ the sort of understanding (Plato here allows it the name of knowledge or science, ἐπιστήμη) appropriate to them; if we want to find the way from one place to another we shall not be helped by knowing the mathematician's straight line, since we could not walk on it: we must know those approximations to straight lines that have thickness and jaggedness.

What is said here is in no way inconsistent with Plato's normal conception of knowledge, save that the actual *word* ἐπιστήμη is extended. His position, now as always, is that sensibles cannot be the objects of exact science, and he normally reserves ἐπιστήμη for the science which deals with non-sensible Forms, using δόξα for the faculty which cognises sensibles and for the state of mind that cannot rise above sensibles. But the whole scheme of the present dialogue, with its parallel classifications of knowledge (cognition) and pleasure, requires the use of a single word to express the generic notion in each case; and ἐπιστήμη, being thus generically used in common speech, has been, next to φρόνησις, the predominant word throughout the dialogue.

It would be foolish to suppose that Plato is now for the first time struck by the thought that you cannot build a house by the light of pure mathematics and nothing else. If he had not pointed this out before, it was because he had no occasion to do so: to emphasise the nature of, and the need for, exact science seemed more important. But now, when it is a question what kinds of cognition, if any, are to be excluded from the good life, the occasion obviously arises.

The discussion of admissible pleasures is thrown into dramatic form, each party, the pleasures and the knowledges, being asked which, if any, of the other 'family' they are willing to live with. This is quite in the Platonic manner, though it goes perhaps a little further than the speech of the personified laws in the *Crito*, or the frequent speeches by the 'argument' (λόγος) itself. So far as it has any purpose beyond increased vivacity in presenting the conclusions we may believe that it is intended to suggest that the 'partners' in the good life live in peace and amity: it will not be a case of a *modus vivendi* imposed from without, but of an agreement by which each factor takes its place in a self-adjusted whole.

The pleasures admitted are enumerated, in the speech of the knowledges, under three heads: (1) the true and pure pleasures previously recognised, (2) those that accompany health and temperance, (3) those that attend upon Virtue in general (συμπάσης ἀρετῆς ὀπαδοί). Earlier (62 E) it has been agreed to admit 'necessary' pleasures, and a comparison with the classification of desires at *Rep.* 558 D ff. makes it probable that these are identical with the second class: they are the pleasures attendant upon the satisfaction of our simple physical needs.[1] The third is a large and vaguely indicated class, and here Plato comes near to the Aristotelian doctrine that the quality of a pleasure, as good or bad, depends on the activity that it attends. It can hardly be doubted that pleasures of this third class are regarded by Plato as good: otherwise they would not find a place in the good life; yet they are expressly distinguished from 'true and pure' pleasures. It is not easy to see why many of our 'activities according to moral goodness' should not produce pleasures which satisfy the condition of purity, viz. of involving either no ἔνδεια or an ἔνδεια ἀναίσθητος (51 B). But the truth probably is that pleasures of this third class, important though they are, cannot really be accommodated to the fundamental Platonic conception of pleasure as πλήρωσις, satisfaction of want or deficiency. That notion is most appropriate in the region of the elementary physical pleasures (i.e. pleasures attendant on the fulfilment of physical needs); it can reasonably be extended, as Plato extends it, to certain kinds of mental pleasure: but there remains the large class of what may be called 'moral pleasures' which Plato has hitherto hardly noticed in our dialogue,[2]

---

[1] *Rep.* 559 A ἆρ' οὖν οὐχ ἡ τοῦ φαγεῖν μέχρι ὑγιείας τε καὶ εὐεξίας καὶ αὐτοῦ σίτου τε καὶ ὄψου ἀναγκαῖος ἂν εἴη (sc. ἐπιθυμία); the Epicureans, building on Plato's ethics, classified desires as (*a*) natural and necessary, (*b*) natural but not necessary, (*c*) neither natural nor necessary, and are said to have ranked sexual desire under (*b*). Plato probably intends this desire, and the corresponding pleasure, as well as those of simple food and drink, to rank as necessary.

[2] It is indeed casually noticed at 12 D ἥδεσθαι δὲ (sc. φαμέν) τὸν σωφρονοῦντα αὐτῷ τῷ σωφρονεῖν.

and which he now notices almost *en passant*. If he had started his investigation of pleasure with these, instead of with the pleasures of food and drink, he would, we may believe, have reached a conception substantially identical with that of Aristotle, of pleasure as the 'supervenient perfection' (ἐπιγινόμενον τέλος, *E.N.* 1174 B 33) of an activity.

Socrates   *Protarchus*

Soc. Come then: to begin with, are we most likely to attain a good 61 D result by mixing all pleasure with all intelligence?

Prot. Possibly.

Soc. No, it's not safe. I think I can show you what seems a less dangerous method of mixture.

Prot. Tell me, please.

Soc. One pleasure, so we thought,[1] had a truer being[2] than another, and again this art was more exact than that?

Prot. Of course.

Soc. And knowledge differed from knowledge: one having regard to the things that come into being and perish, the other to those that E do not come into being nor perish, but are always, unchanged and unaltered. Reviewing them on the score of truth, we concluded that the latter was truer than the former.

Prot. Perfectly right.

Soc. Then if we were to see which were the truest portions of each before we made our mixture,[3] would the fusion of these portions suffice to constitute and provide us with the fully acceptable life, or should we still need something different?

Prot. My own opinion is that we should act as you say.   62

Soc. Now let us imagine a man who understands what Justice itself is, and can give an account of it conformable to his knowledge, and who moreover has a like understanding of all else that is.

Prot. Very well.

Soc. Will such a man be adequately possessed of knowledge, if he can give his account of the divine[4] circle, and the divine sphere them-

---

[1] I accept φόμεθα (Richards) for οἰόμεθα in D 7.

[2] I.e. 'was less of a γένεσις, nearer to an οὐσία', than another. Not 'was truer', for ἦν ἀληθῶς μᾶλλον could not mean that: though ultimately the two things come to the same. Socrates has not actually said this already, but he came near to it at 52 C-D.

[3] If συμμείξαντες is correct, the time of the aorist participle must be the same as that of ἴδοιμεν. This use is common enough, but a better sense would be given by συμμείξοντες, and I have translated accordingly.

[4] For θεῖος used of an Idea, cf. *Soph.* 254 B and Cornford, *PTK*, p. 190, note 3.

selves, but knows nothing of these human spheres and circles of ours, so that, when he is building a house, the rules that he uses, no less than
B the circles, are of the other sort?[1]

Prot. I am moved to mirth, Socrates, by this description we are giving of ourselves confined to divine knowledge.

Soc. What's that? Are we to throw in alongside of our other ingredients the art of the false rule and false circle, with all the lack of fixity and purity it involves?

Prot. We must, if we are going to find the way home when we want it.

C *Soc.* And music too, which we said a while ago was so completely dependent on lucky shots and imitation, and so deficient in purity?

Prot. I think we are bound to do so, if our life is ever to be a life at all.

Soc. Do you want me, may I ask, to give way like a porter jostled and knocked about by the crowd, to fling open the doors and allow every sort of knowledge to stream in, the inferior mingling with the pure?

D *Prot.* I don't really see, Socrates, what harm one would suffer by taking all those other sorts of knowledge, providing one had the first sort.

Soc. Then I am to allow the whole company to stream in and be gathered together in a splendid Homeric mingling of the waters?[2]

Prot. Certainly.

Soc. It is done. And now we must return to our fount of pleasures. The method of mixing our ingredients[3] which we intended, namely taking parts of the true sorts first, has broken down: our acquiescence in every sort of knowledge has made us admit the whole of it at one
E swoop before admitting any pleasure.

Prot. That is quite true.

Soc. Hence it is time for us to raise the same question about pleasures, whether we are to let them all loose at once or should allow passage first to such of them as are true.

Prot. It is most important in the interest of safety to let loose the true ones first.

---

[1] I take χρώμενος not as concessive but as conditional, parallel to ἀγνοῶν. τοῖς ἄλλοις means the 'divine' sort, and ὁμοίως is added because κανόνες have not yet been mentioned, whereas κύκλοι have.
[2] The reference is to *Iliad* IV, 452 ff.
[3] αὐτά (Apelt) for αὐτάς in D 8 seems necessary, for αὐτάς could only mean ἡδονάς, which is not what the sense requires.

Soc. Then let that be taken as done. And what next? Ought we not to do as we did in the other case, and include in our mixture any necessary pleasures there may be?

Prot. O yes, the necessary ones of course.

Soc. Yes, but we found it harmless and useful to spend our lives in 63 the knowledge of all the arts: and if we say the same about pleasures, if, that is, it is advantageous and harmless to us all to spend our lives in the enjoyment of all pleasures, then we must mix in all of them.

Prot. Then what are we to say on this particular point? How are we to act?

Soc. The question ought to be addressed not to us, Protarchus, but to the pleasures themselves and the intelligences; and here is the sort of enquiry we should make about their mutual relations.

Prot. Yes?   B

Soc. 'Dear Pleasures—if that is the name by which I should call you, or whatever it ought to be[1]—would you not choose to live in company with all Intelligence rather than apart from any?' I imagine there can be no doubt about the reply they would make to that.

Prot. What would it be?

Soc. Conformably to what was previously said, it would be as follows: 'It is disadvantageous and hardly possible that one family[2] should be kept in solitude and isolation, perfectly clear of all others; but our view is that, family for family, we cannot do better than have c the family of knowledge to live with us, knowledge of all things in general and of each of ourselves in particular to the fullest extent possible.'[3]

Prot. 'An excellent answer that', we shall tell them.

Soc. So we should. Then next we must put a question to Intelligence and Reason: 'Do you require any pleasures to be added to the mixture?

[1] As Bury remarks, the offer of a choice of title is proper in addressing divinities: compare 12 C. The suggestion is that, in spite of the existence of good pleasures, the word 'pleasure' has perhaps undesirable associations; by Plato himself it has usually been applied to the 'lower' kinds of bodily satisfaction. It was from a wish to get rid of these associations that the Stoics allowed their sage not ἡδονή but χαρά (Diog. Laert. VII, 116). Compare also Prodicus's distinction between εὐφραίνεσθαι and ἥδεσθαι at *Protag.* 337 C.

[2] γένος here probably means both *family* and *kind* or *class* in the logical sense, and there is an allusion to the doctrine of κοινωνία γενῶν (εἰδῶν) at *Soph.* 251 D ff.

[3] The language here is difficult, and the text possibly corrupt; but the general meaning seems to be that the several kinds or 'families' (γένη) of pleasure will each choose as its associate the kind of knowledge appropriate to control it, though knowledge of 'things in general' (τἆλλα πάντα) must be involved in such control.

And when we ask that of Reason and Intelligence, they may possibly rejoin 'What sort of pleasures?'

Prot. I daresay.

D *Soc.* To which our rejoinder is this: 'Over and above the true pleasures that you know of, do you further require the greatest and intensest pleasures for your associates?' And they may well reply: 'Is that likely, Socrates, seeing that they put countless obstacles in our way, disturbing with frenzy the souls in which we dwell, and prevent E us from ever coming into existence: while as to our offspring, they utterly ruin them in most cases, so careless and forgetful do they make us. No: the pleasures you have spoken of as true and pure you may regard as more or less related to us; and besides them you may add to the mixture those that consort with health and temperance, and in fact all that attend upon virtue in general, following her everywhere as their divinity. But to mix with Reason the pleasures that always go with folly and all other manner of evil would surely be the most senseless act for one who desired to see a mixture and fusion as fair 64 and peaceable as might be, so that he might try to learn from it what the Good is, in man and in the universe, and what form he should divine it to possess.'[1] Shall we not say that in the words that Reason has here used it has answered wisely and reason-ably[2] on behalf of itself and memory and right opinion?

Prot. Completely so.

64 A–66 A   *Goodness is revealed in the Mixed Life under three forms, Beauty, Proportion and Truth, to each of which Intelligence is more akin than Pleasure*

This section begins with a puzzling demand for the inclusion of reality (ἀλήθεια) in the mixture; without that, we are told, 'a thing will never come into being, and if it did it would not continue in being'.

Socrates leaves this unexplained, and we cannot help wondering, first how reality can possibly be an ingredient in the mixture, and secondly if it—or truth—is not already in the mixture as containing true pleasures (though, we must remember, alongside of some which

---

[1] The language of this speech is very reminiscent of what is said about bodily desires and pleasures at *Phaedo* 65–67. Compare especially 65 A, τί δὲ δὴ περὶ αὐτὴν τὴν τῆς φρονήσεως κτῆσιν; πότερον ἐμπόδιον τὸ σῶμα ἢ οὔ, ἐάν τις αὐτὸ ἐν τῇ ζητήσει κοινωνὸν συμπαραλαμβάνῃ; 66 C, ἔτι δέ, ἄν τινες νόσοι προσπέσωσιν, ἐμποδίζουσιν ἡμῶν τὴν τοῦ ὄντος θήραν; 66 D, ἐκ τούτου (sc. τοῦ σώματος) ἀσχολίαν ἄγομεν φιλοσοφίας πέρι, *ibid.* ἐν ταῖς ζητήσεσιν αὖ πανταχοῦ παραπῖπτον (sc. τὸ σῶμα) θόρυβον παρέχει καὶ ταραχὴν καὶ ἐκπλήττει; 67 A, ἀπαλλαττόμενοι τῆς τοῦ σώματος ἀφροσύνης.

[2] ἐχόντως ἑαυτόν (A 2) is a quasi-punning substitute for νουνεχόντως, 'sensibly'.

are not true, as we saw in the last section) and true knowledges (also alongside of knowledges which are not fully true).

Plato is, it would seem, giving quasi-humorous expression to a passing doubt. Is the good life, which we have spent so much labour on discovering, capable of being actually lived? Or is it, as Glaucon fears the Ideal State may be, at the end of *Republic* IX, a mere philosophers' fantasy (ἐν λόγοις κείμενον)? What Socrates says here should not be taken literally; if our mixed life is a mere fantasy we cannot turn it into a real existent by, as it were, pumping reality into it. Rather it is Plato's way of expressing his hope and faith that the kind of life indicated is no impossible ideal, and his recognition that unless it is so all his labour in the dialogue has been vain.

To interpret the passage thus is compatible with what we learn a page or so later (64 E–65 A), that Reality is one of the three 'notes' of Goodness. However beautiful and tidy a scheme may be on paper, it is quite valueless if it cannot be given actuality.

The other two notes of Goodness, or 'forms in which we can hunt down the good' (65 A) are Beauty and Proportion,[1] and the discussion implies that these are so closely interdependent that they can hardly be distinguished. That the goodness of any mixture must be due to its 'measure and symmetry' is declared to be obvious; and of course the close connexion of goodness with beauty, and of beauty with proportion between the parts of a whole, is too familiar both in Plato and in Greek thought in general to need illustrating. And it should be remembered that we have been prepared for this line of thought by an earlier passage of our dialogue, in which all good conditions, whether in nature or in man, were said to be due to the mixture of Limit and Unlimited, and the third 'kind' to result from the '*measures* achieved with the aid of the Limit' (ἐκ τῶν μετὰ τοῦ πέρατος ἀπειργασμένων μέτρων, 26 D). We are now, it appears, in a position to test the respective affinities of the two claimants, Intelligence (Reason) and Pleasure, to confirm at last what Socrates said early in the dialogue: 'this is the point for which I will contend with Philebus even more warmly than before: that whatever it is which, by its inclusion in this mixed life, makes that life both desirable and good, it is something to which reason is nearer and more akin than pleasure' (22 D).

As the first point of comparison we take ἀλήθεια. Since 64 B this word has meant 'reality' rather than 'truth', but, as Dr Bury reminds us,[2] these are in fact the objective and subjective sides of a single notion. There is therefore no real shift of meaning when the ἀλήθεια of reason is now contrasted with the bragging imposture of pleasure, which is declared to be 'the worst of all impostors' (ἁπάντων ἀλαζονίστατον).

---

[1] Socrates speaks of μέτρον καὶ ἡ σύμμετρος φύσις at 64 D, of μετριότης καὶ συμμετρία at 64 E, of συμμετρία at 65 A, and of μετριότης at 65 B. It seems probable that the two pairs and the two single nouns are for the present to be regarded as all equivalent, though later (66 A) a distinction will be drawn.

[2] Appendix F, pp. 201 ff.

But we do inevitably ask ourselves whether this summary condemnation is fair, and consistent with the recognition of pure pleasures, necessary pleasures, and pleasures attendant upon virtue in general (63 E)—and indeed with the fundamental notion of the dialogue, that some pleasures rightly take their place in the good life, and are therefore at least in some sense good. Let it be granted that *some* pleasures merit this condemnation: but have they not been expressly excluded from the mixture, and ought they not therefore to be disregarded in answering our present question, which part of the mixture is more akin to that which makes it good?

Our answer must, I think, be that, so far as any pleasure has been approved in the dialogue, it has been because of something outside itself which has modified its nature, and in particular has checked its innate tendency to indefinite increase. We may recall once more the emphatic statement at 31 A: 'pleasure is itself unlimited and belongs to the kind that does not and never will contain *within itself and derived from itself* either beginning, or middle, or end'. Whether we say that it is Reason or Limit that modifies the nature of ἡδονὴ αὐτή matters little, when we remember that all the μέτρα that characterise good μεικτά are μετὰ τοῦ πέρατος ἀπειργασμένα by the causality of νοῦς. But the essential point is that for the purpose of our judgment between pleasure and reason we are entitled, and indeed compelled, to regard all pleasures, even those approved and admitted, in abstraction from reason. The difficulty arises from the fact that the imagery of a mixture makes us think of two quite distinct components, or sets of components; whereas in fact one component (the approved pleasures) is already 'mixed' with the other (reason) before entering into the mixture. We may call this confused thinking if we like: and for my own part I think that the conception of a mixed life, natural as it is, is not the best and easiest method for comparing the intrinsic values of pleasure and intelligence; but Plato's doctrine is really quite clear, namely that because such value as any pleasure has is due to its association with Reason and Limit, therefore it is an inferior, though a necessary, factor in the good life.

In our determination of the various sorts of mixed or impure pleasures we were in fact discovering various characters attaching to ἡδονὴ αὐτή, to pleasure *qua* unlimited and unassociated with reason. And one of these characters (though it did not receive the name at the time) was imposture, ἀλαζονεία, the pretence of being worth more than you really are. All three types of pleasure discriminated in the long discussion from 36 C to 44 A are impostors.

After ἀλήθεια Socrates next (65 D) declares that reason has more μετριότης than pleasure. This needs no further comment after what has been said.

As to the third 'note' of Goodness, Beauty, the inferiority of pleasure is based on the fact that some pleasures are admittedly ugly or shameful (αἰσχρά), whereas no one has ever so conceived intelligence. This strikes us as hardly more than a rhetorical appeal to anti-hedonist prejudice. Probably Plato does not intend it to be taken as a serious argument, but feels that the absence of μετριότης necessarily involves the absence of κάλλος. The real purpose and effect of this last piece of the argument is to bring out the *moral* ugliness involved in the 'unlimitedness' of pleasure.

Socrates   Protarchus

Soc. But there is still a certain thing we must have, and nothing in 64A the world could come into being without it.

Prot. What is that?   B

Soc. Reality: for a thing with which we don't mean to mix reality will never really come into being, and if it ever did it wouldn't continue in being.

Prot. No, of course not.

Soc. No indeed. And now do you and Philebus tell me if there are any additional ingredients required. To me it appears that in our present discussion we have created what might be called an incorporeal ordered system[1] for the rightful control of a corporeal subject in which dwells a soul.

Prot. You may assure yourself, Socrates, that my own conclusion is the same.

Soc. Then perhaps we should be more or less right in saying that we now stand upon the threshold of the Good and of that habitation c where all that is like thereto resides?[2]

Prot. I at least think so.

Soc. And what, may I ask, shall we regard as the most valuable thing in our mixture, that which makes an arrangement of this sort commend itself to us all? If we discover that, we can go on to consider whether this factor in the whole scheme of things[3] is closer and more akin to pleasure, or to reason.

[1] The word κόσμος is intended to suggest the regular Pythagorean and Platonic comparison of macrocosm and microcosm, and the ethical doctrine that we must reproduce in ourselves the order of the universe. Cf. *Gorgias* 508 A; *Timaeus* 47 C, 90 D.

[2] I retain, with some doubt, καὶ and τῆς τοῦ τοιούτου which Badham and Burnet bracket in c 2. Socrates seems to distinguish αὐτὸ τὸ ἀγαθόν and those Forms which are most ἀγαθοειδῆ.

[3] By ἐν τῷ παντί Socrates indicates that we must extend our purview from man to the universe. Proportion and Beauty and Truth are akin to the Reason in the world-soul, as well as to the reason in our own souls. The same point is made in the words ἐν ἀνθρώποις τε καὶ θεοῖς at 65 B.

D   *Prot.* Very good: what you propose will do much to help us towards our decision.

Soc. As a matter of fact, it is easy enough to see the cause that makes any mixture, be it what it may, possess high value or no value whatever.

Prot. How so?

Soc. Surely anyone in the world can recognise that.

Prot. Recognise what?

Soc. That any compound, whatever it be, that does not by some means or other exhibit measure and proportion, is the ruin both of its ingredients and, first and foremost, of itself; what you are bound to E get in such cases is no real mixture, but literally a miserable mass of unmixed messiness.[1]

Prot. Very true.

Soc. So now we find that the Good has taken refuge in the character of the Beautiful: for the qualities of measure and proportion invariably, I imagine, constitute beauty and excellence.

Prot. Yes indeed.

Soc. And of course we said that truth was included along with these qualities in the mixture.

Prot. Quite so.

65   *Soc.* Then if we cannot hunt down the Good under a single form, let us secure it by the conjunction of three, Beauty, Proportion, and Truth; and then, regarding these three as one, let us assert that *that* may most properly be held to determine the qualities of the mixture, and that because *that* is good the mixture itself has become so.

Prot. Yes, that is quite proper.

Soc. Well, Protarchus, by this time anyone would be competent to B decide whether it is pleasure or intelligence that is more akin to the highest Good, and more valuable with men and gods alike.

Prot. The answer is clear, but for all that it would be as well to formulate it explicitly.

Soc. Then let us examine each of our three forms separately in relation to pleasure and reason; for we must see to which of the two we shall assign each of them on the ground of closer kinship.

Prot. By 'each of them' you mean Beauty, Truth and Measuredness?

Soc. Yes; and in the first place, Protarchus, take hold of Truth; and

[1] The Greek contains a pun on the etymological and the ordinary meanings of συμφορά: 'what is brought together' (lump) and 'calamity'

having done so, have a look at the three things, Reason, Truth and c
Pleasure; and then, taking your time, answer your own question
whether Pleasure or Reason is the more akin to Truth.

Prot. What need for time? I think they differ widely. Pleasure is
the worst of all impostors, and according to the accounts, when it is
a question of the pleasures of love, which are commonly reckoned as
the greatest, even perjury is forgiven by the gods;[1] pleasures being
presumably, like children, completely destitute of Reason. Reason, on D
the other hand, if not identical with Truth, is of all things the most like
it, the truest thing in the world.

Soc. Next then give a similar consideration to Measuredness; has
pleasure more of it than intelligence, or is the reverse the case?

Prot. There you set me another easy problem to consider. I don't
think you could discover anything whatsoever more unmeasured in its
character than pleasure and intense enjoyment, nor anything more
measured than reason and knowledge.

Soc. Well said. However, there is still a third thing I want you to E
tell me. Has Reason more part in Beauty than Pleasure, that is to say
is Reason more beautiful than Pleasure, or is the opposite the case?

Prot. Well, of course, Socrates, no one whether in his waking hours
or in his dreams has had a vision of Intelligence and Reason as ugly:
no one can ever possibly have conceived them as being or becoming
ugly, or ever going to be so.

Soc. Right.

Prot. But I fancy that when we see someone, no matter whom,
experiencing pleasures—and I think this is true especially of the
greatest pleasures—we detect in them an element either of the ridiculous
or of extreme ugliness, so that we ourselves feel ashamed, and do our 66
best to cover it up and hide it away: and we leave that sort of thing to
the hours of darkness, feeling that it should not be exposed to the
light of day.

66 A–67 B   *Fivefold classification of goods, in which pleasures are
relegated to the lowest place*

Socrates now proceeds, on the basis of the whole preceding discussion,
to arrange the 'possessions' of mankind in a scale of decreasing value.
Apart from a serious textual problem in the first sentence, the passage
is perhaps not so difficult or mysterious as has been usually supposed.

[1] Compare (with Bury) *Symp.* 183 B.

The first κτῆμα is said to be 'in the region of' μέτρον καὶ τὸ μέτριον καὶ καίριον and so forth, the second in that of τὸ σύμμετρον καὶ καλὸν καὶ τὸ τέλεον καὶ ἱκανόν and so forth.

Plato evidently means that in the good life the highest value belongs, not to its ingredients, but to its *form*;[1] for, as we have seen, it is in its form that its goodness really lies. That goodness has been declared to be apprehensible in the three aspects of κάλλος συμμετρία and ἀλήθεια, the first two of which have been treated as so closely interdependent as to be hardly distinguishable, while the second has, to all appearance, been used interchangeably with μετριότης. Now however we get (*a*) a discrimination between μέτρον and σύμμετρον, (*b*) a collocation of καλόν with σύμμετρον, and (*c*) an absence of any mention of ἀλήθεια.

Let us then seek the reason for (*a*): this is, in effect, to ask how the first κτῆμα differs from the second. The difference, I suggest, lies mainly in this, that in the formula of the first we are looking at each part or factor of the good life by itself, so that the formula signifies the achievement of right quantitative determination in respect of each knowledge and each pleasure. (Plato is no doubt thinking mainly, if not exclusively, of the μέτρα imposed on pleasures: that any kind of knowledge can go to excess he has never suggested.) In the formula of the second we look at the good life as a whole, or (which is the same thing) we apprehend the relations of its parts. Thus it is natural enough that καίριον should occur in the first: for καιρός is the *point* of rightness, not something spread out, so to speak, over the parts of a whole; it is natural too that the second κτῆμα should be second, since the rightness of inter-related parts is logically posterior to the rightness of each part. As between first and second, the order is, I think, not really ethical but logical.

It may be noted that at *Statesman* 284 E, where the Eleatic Stranger is discriminating two sorts of μετρητική, that namely which is purely relative and that which has reference to a norm, a sentence occurs very similar to the first formula both in terminology and structure: ὁπόσαι (sc. τέχναι μετροῦσι) πρὸς τὸ μέτριον καὶ τὸ πρέπον καὶ τὸν καιρὸν καὶ τὸ δέον καὶ πάνθ' ὁπόσα εἰς τὸ μέσον ἀπῳκίσθη τῶν ἐσχάτων.[2]

As to (*b*), little need be said. The beauty of a whole is plainly due to the relation of its parts, and will therefore be ranged alongside τὸ σύμμετρον rather than τὸ μέτριον when these are distinguished.

To come to (*c*), the omission of ἀλήθεια is certainly puzzling, and I can offer no more than a tentative solution. I dissent from the suggestion that it is covertly or ambiguously introduced under the *third* κτῆμα, in the words οὐκ ἂν μέγα τι τῆς ἀληθείας παρεξέλθοις.

---

[1] So Bury, App. F, p. 209: 'The first two grades…contain mention not of constituent factors but of conditions or formal causes, the elements themselves being first brought in with the third group.'

[2] Souilhé (*La notion platonicienne d'intermédiaire*, p. 34) reminds us of the prominence of the notion of καιρός in the Hippocratic writings: 'le grand rôle de la médecine est-il de découvrir le καιρός, ce point exact qui établit dans le corps un parfait équilibre et l'aide à triompher des éléments perturbateurs'.

These words have, I believe, no more than their natural meaning: 'you won't be far out' (i.e. 'you will be quite right'); ἀλήθεια, if it is to be mentioned at all, would surely be mentioned as a form, not as an ingredient: and the third formula is of ingredients. Now the phrasing τὸ σύμμετρον καὶ καλὸν καὶ τὸ τέλεον καὶ ἱκανόν implies, by its articles, two pairs of qualities, and it may be that Plato feels that by the second pair, 'perfect and adequate', he is expressing his meaning as well as, or better than, if he had written τὸ ἀληθές. The two adjectives were used earlier (20 D) along with αἱρετός to express certain essential characters of the good life; τέλεος we there interpreted by its connexion with τέλος: the good life must be such as we can make an *end*, a completely satisfying goal of endeavour; while ἱκανός reinforced this character: such a life will be adequate, as needing no supplement. But what is thus perfect and adequate will necessarily be 'true', in the sense of expressing the *idea*[1] or ideal of human life; perfection is 'truth to type', imperfection is failure to be true to type. Hence τὸ τέλεον and τὸ ἱκανόν may be fairly said to be 'notes' of Truth, just as Beauty, Proportion and Truth were found to be 'notes' of Goodness.

The third and fourth possessions present no difficulty. νοῦς and φρόνησις, as the faculties cognisant of the highest reality, are here, conformably with what was said at 59 D, discriminated from the lower types of cognition, 'sciences and arts and true judgments'; though, as we saw above, Plato has not elsewhere in the dialogue found it necessary to make this distinction.

Fifthly, we have the pure (unmixed, true) pleasures, and a somewhat ambiguous mention of a sixth class is probably a way of providing for the two other sorts of pleasure admitted at 63 E.

The classification is followed by a formal recapitulation of the main argument, and the dialogue ends with an emphatic declaration which recalls Philebus's initial appeal to 'all creatures' (11 B): pleasure has taken fifth place in the scale of human values, in spite of what we are told by 'all the oxen and horses and other beasts and every other animal that exists'.

Socrates Protarchus Philebus

Soc. Then your message, Protarchus, to be sent out to the world 66 A at large and announced to your immediate listeners, will be this: Pleasure is not the first of all possessions, not yet the second; rather, the first has been secured for everlasting tenure somewhere in the region of measure—of what is measured or appropriate, or whatever term may be deemed to denote the quality in question.[2]

Prot. So at least it appears on our present showing.

---

[1] Cf. Bury, p. 204: 'A thing is ἀληθές when it is what it *is*, when it expresses its own proper τί ἐστί or οὐσία.'

[2] For a defence of the reading τὴν ἀίδιον ᾑρῆσθαι, and of the interpretation here adopted, I may refer to a note in *C.Q.* January 1939, pp. 28–29. I take τὴν ἀίδιον as a cognate accusative (=τὴν ἀίδιον αἵρεσιν), and ᾑρῆσθαι as passive.

B   *Soc.* And the second lies in the region of what is proportioned and beautiful, and what is perfect and satisfying and so forth—whatever terms denote that kind of quality.

Prot. That seems right.

Soc. And if you accept what I divine, and put reason and intelligence third, you won't be very wide of the truth.

Prot. Perhaps not.

Soc. Nor again,[1] if beside these three you put as fourth what we recognised as belonging to the soul itself, sciences and arts and what
C we called right opinions, inasmuch as these are more akin than Pleasure to the Good.

Prot. You may be right.

Soc. And as fifth, the pleasures which we recognised and dis-criminated as painless, calling them pure pleasures of the soul itself:[2] some of them attaching to knowledge, others to sensation.

Prot. Perhaps so.

Soc. 'But cease at sixth descent', as Orpheus puts it, 'your ordered song'; really it looks as though our discussion, like the song, has ceased at the sixth choice.[3] And now the only thing left for us to do
D is to crown our story with a capital.

Prot. That is what we must do.

Soc. Come along then, let us have the 'third libation to the Deliverer', and repeat for the third time the same pronouncement that we made before.

Prot. What is that?

Soc. Philebus maintained that we find the Good in the sum-total and entirety of pleasure.

Prot. I understand you, Socrates, to have meant by your 'third libation' just now that we were to recapitulate our original statement.

---

[1] I accept Jackson's οὐδ' for οὐ τέταρτα in B 8.

[2] All pleasures are of course psychical experiences, but some may be said to belong to the soul in a special sense, namely that they do not originate in physical processes of depletion and replenishment (cf. 32 B ff.). The pure pleasures attaching to sensation (51 B) are amongst these, although they involve the bodily sense-organs.

[3] This Orphic verse is otherwise unknown, though Plutarch quotes it from the present passage at *E ap. Delph.* 391 D (with οἶμον for κόσμον). The 'sixth class' must presumably be that of the other admitted pleasures mentioned at 63 E: but Plato seems to be suggesting that, since these have only been noticed very cursorily in the discussion, he will leave them out as virtually 'not classed' (or perhaps we should say 'not candidates for honours'). It is possible (as at 23 D) that he may be affected by a predilection for the number 5, as Plutarch suggests in this connexion (*ibid.*).

Soc. Yes, and let us listen to what came next. I, having in view the E considerations which I have now detailed, and feeling distaste for the assertion which is not only that of Philebus but also frequently made by countless other people, maintained that reason is far better and more valuable than pleasure for human life.

Prot. So you did.

Soc. Moreover, while suspecting that many other things are so too,[1] I said that if anything were to come to light that was better than both of these I should fight to the end on the side of Reason against Pleasure for the second prize, and that Pleasure would be disappointed even of that.

Prot. Yes, you did say so.   67

Soc. And subsequently we were completely satisfied that neither of them was satisfying.

Prot. Very true.

Soc. Then in that part of our argument had Reason and Pleasure alike been dismissed as being, neither of them, the Good itself, inasmuch as they came short of self-sufficiency and the quality of being satisfying and perfect?

Prot. Quite right.

Soc. But now that we have found a third thing better than either of them, Reason has been found ever so much nearer and more akin than Pleasure to the character of the victor.[2]

Prot. Certainly.

Soc. Then according to the decision now pronounced by our argument, Pleasure will take fifth place.

Prot. Apparently.

Soc. And not first place, no, not even if all the oxen and horses and B every other animal that exists tell us so by their pursuit of pleasure.[3] It is the animals on which the multitude rely, just as diviners rely on birds, when they decide that pleasures are of the first importance to

---

[1] εἶναι in E 7 means ἡδονῆς βελτίονά τε καὶ ἀμείνονα εἶναι. Socrates did not suspect that there were many things better than *both* Pleasure *and* Intelligence. These ἄλλα πολλά are no doubt the lower forms of cognition, discriminated from νοῦς and φρόνησις and placed in the fourth class at 66 B, and referred to as δόξα ὀρθή καὶ ἀληθεῖς λογισμοί at 11 B.

[2] The ἰδέα τοῦ νικῶντος is the goodness of the good life, distinguished from τἀγαθὸν αὐτό above (A 6), which means the actual thing (life) which has 'good' predicated of it. At 61 A on the other hand τἀγαθόν must mean goodness (the Form of Good), as we saw on p. 122 above.

[3] Philebus had at the very outset maintained that pleasure is the good for all creatures (πᾶσι ζῴοις, 11 B).

our living a good life, and suppose that animals' desires are authoritative evidence, rather than those desires that are known to reasoned argument,[1] divining the truth of this and that by the power of the Muse of Philosophy.

Prot. The point has been reached, Socrates, at which we all agree that your conclusions are completely true.

Soc. Then will you let me go?

Prot. There is only a little still left to be done, Socrates. I am sure you won't give up sooner than we do, so I will remind you of the tasks that remain.[2]

ADDITIONAL NOTE

on 'Collection' (συναγωγή)

Since writing my comment on p. 26, I have come to the conclusion, chiefly as the result of a fresh study of the *Sophist*, that my account of συναγωγή needs correction. I have there followed what is, I think, the commonly accepted view, that Collection is (*a*) always Collection of kinds (species), never of particulars, and (*b*) a process to be completed before Division starts: once Division has started, Collection plays no more part in dialectic method. Both (*a*) and (*b*) are stated or implied by Cornford[3] and Stenzel-Allan;[4] other writers known to me have indeed differed as to (*a*): for example Von Arnim, who, summarising the formal account of dialectic given at *Phaedrus* 265 D, writes "Das erste dieser beiden εἴδη, die zusammen nach 266c die Kunst des Dialektikers ausmachen, ist das Zusammenschauen (συνορῶντα) und Verbinden (ἄγειν) der vielfältig zerstreuten Einzelheiten (τὰ πολλαχῇ διεσπαρμένα) in die Einheit des Begriffs"[5]): on (*b*) however I have found no dissentient opinion.

It can hardly be denied that the words τὰ πολλαχῇ διεσπαρμένα are most naturally taken as referring to particulars, and that Hermeias (p. 234, Couvreur) was right in connecting the sentence in which they occur—εἰς μίαν ἰδέαν συνορῶντα ἄγειν τὰ πολλαχῇ διεσπαρμένα—with

---

[1] λόγων is difficult. The parallel genitives θηρίων and λόγων must be possessive; but if desires can be properly said to 'belong' to arguments in any sense, it cannot be in the same sense in which they belong to animals. I suggest (tentatively) λόγῳ, which would give a natural contrast between the desires of animals and the desires of *persons* who, by following the Muse of Philosophy, have divined truth through reasoned argument.

[2] The reference is doubtless to the further discussion of mixed pleasures promised for to-morrow at 50 D.

[3] *PTK*, pp. 170, 186.

[4] *Plato's Method of Dialectic*, Introduction, p. xvi.

[5] *Platos Jugenddialoge*, p. 198. Similarly Raeder (*Platons phil. Entwickelung*, p. 261), "die verschiedenen Phänomene zu eine Einheit zusammenfassen".

an earlier passage of the *Phaedrus* (249 B), δεῖ γὰρ ἄνθρωπον συνιέναι κατ' εἶδος λεγόμενον, ἐκ πολλῶν ἰὸν αἰσθήσεων εἰς ἓν λογισμῷ συναιρούμενον. On the other hand it is true that the Divisional schemes of the *Sophist* and *Statesman*, in so far as they show traces of Collection at all, appear never to envisage a Collection of particulars into an εἶδος; while *Philebus* 16 C–D, δεῖν οὖν ἡμᾶς τούτων οὕτω διακεκοσμημένων ἀεὶ μίαν ἰδέαν περὶ παντὸς ἑκάστοτε θεμένους ζητεῖν, εὑρήσειν γὰρ ἔνουσαν, is ambiguous on the point.

It seems simplest to conclude that Plato means us always to think of the Forms mentioned in a Collection (e.g. the various kinds gathered together into διακριτικὴ τέχνη at *Soph.* 226 B–C) as reached by a previous Collection of particulars, since it is in fact, according to the *Phaedrus* doctrine, only thus that they can be reached: but that he does not deem it necessary to remind us of this. In this sense, then, and with this proviso, it remains true that συναγωγή (equally with διαίρεσις) is not concerned with particulars.

Examination of the Divisions in the *Sophist* seems to reveal that a Collection is made at many stages of the process. At 219 A–C there are clear Collections of the two kinds of Art, Productive and Acquisitive; at 220 C, where Fishing is divided into fishing by enclosure and fishing by striking, the former kind is reached by a Collection of varieties of enclosure (κύρτους δὴ καὶ δίκτυα. . . .ἕρκη χρὴ προσαγορεύειν). Sometimes, perhaps more often, the Collection is thinly disguised as a *description* of a kind ostensibly reached by Division alone; thus at 223 E Export Trading (ἐμπορική) is divided into that concerned with bodily needs and that concerned with needs of the soul; and the Stranger, realizing that Theaetetus will not grasp the notion of psychical commodities, describes or catalogues them, thus making it clear that ψυχεμπορική is a kind that has been reached, and can only be reached, by a Collection of its own kinds.

But probably the most convincing evidence that Collection has its place within (and not merely before) a scheme of Division occurs at 267 A–B. Here Semblance-making (τὸ φανταστικόν) is divided into Mimicry and τὸ δι' ὀργάνων γιγνόμενον: and the Stranger excuses himself from collecting and naming the latter kind in these words: "Let us reserve that section, then, under the name of mimicry, and indulge ourselves so far as to leave all the rest for someone else to collect into a unity (συναγαγεῖν εἰς ἕν) and give it an appropriate name" (Cornford's translation).

INDEX OF PROPER NAMES

Adam, J., 87
Alcmaeon, 58
Alexander Polyhistor, 42
Anaxagoras, 50
Antisthenes, 17, 31
Apelt, O., 52, 66, 79, 87, 92, 118, 130
Archer-Hind, R. D., 20
Aristotle, 4, 6, 7, 12, 13, 17, 32, 37, 41–3, 61, 72, 82, 86, 87, 92, 100, 106, 107, 113, 117, 120

Badham, C., 47, 57, 62, 80, 117, 135
Bäumker, C., 2
Bekker, I., 52, 58, 118
Bosanquet, B., 99
Burnet, J., 16, 47, 60, 65, 82, 86, 91, 94, 104, 108, 135
Bury, J. B., 20
Bury, R. G., 2, 13, 20, 39, 47–9, 56, 58, 65, 76, 78, 83, 92, 106, 118, 131, 133, 137–9

Callicles, 6, 8, 58, 107, 111
Clement, 82
Cornford, F. M., 2–4, 7, 17, 21, 31, 39, 126, 129

Democritus, 87, 121
Diès, A., 50
Diogenes of Apollonia, 50
Diogenes Laertius, 42, 131
Dion, 1, 3, 4
Dionysius II, 1, 2, 4

Empedocles, 44, 59
Eudoxus, 4, 5, 6, 12

Friedländer, P., 6, 20, 75, 88

Gellius, Aulus, 4
Gorgias, 113, 120–1
Grote, G., 87, 116
Grube, G. M. A., 49

Hermocrates, 3
Hipparinus, 3
Homer, 130

Jackson, H., 2, 15, 104, 140

Karpp, H., 6

Lucian, 6

Mauersberger, A., 108
Mill, J. S., 116
Moore, G. E., 32, 123

Paley, F. A., 52
Philistion, 3
Plotinus, 123
Plutarch, 37, 44, 140
Proclus, 57
Prodicus, 131
Prometheus, 21, 23
Protagoras, 86
Pythagoras, 21

Raeder, H., 3, 7
Richards, H., 129
Ritter, C., 92, 103
Ross, W. D., 39, 40

Schleiermacher, F. D., 60, 116
Skemp, J. B., 12.
Souilhé, J., 88, 138
Speusippus, 4, 5, 13, 82, 83, 87, 108, 111
Stallbaum, G., 18, 75

Taylor, A. E., 2, 3, 6, 39, 41, 58, 67, 87, 92–3, 99, 110, 113
Theaetetus, 1
Timaeus, 7

Vahlen, J., 47

Xenophon, 50

Zeller, E., 39, 57